BRIGHT SPARKS

© ALISTAIR SMITH
ISBN 1-85539-088-4

Production by AL!TE
45 Wycombe End, Beaconsfield, Bucks HP9 1LZ

All rights reserved. No part of this publication may be reproduced, stored in a retrieval system or reproduced or transmitted in any form or by any means, electronic, mechanical, photocopying – excepting single copies which may be made for use in the purchasing institution, recording or otherwise, without the prior written permission of the publishers. This book may not be lent, resold, hired out or otherwise disposed of by way of trade in any form of binding or cover other than that in which it is published, without the prior consent of the publishers.

Every effort has been made to contact copyright holders of materials reproduced in this book. The publishers apologize for any omissions and will be pleased to rectify them at the earliest opportunity.

Design and Layout: Neil Hawkins
Published by: Network Educational Press Ltd
Illustrations: Oliver Caviglioli
Printed in Great Britain by MPG Books Ltd

visit the website   www.alite.co.uk

BRIGHT SPARKS

an introduction

This book of posters for pupils is for teachers and for parents to use to help children learn. Each poster has been carefully chosen and carefully positioned within the book. The posters come from different sources. Some are observations about learning based on my own work and put into sayings children can easily understand and remember. Some are from people researching into the workings of the human brain. Some are quotes from famous people. I have tried to use either famous people who the children may know and admire, or very famous figures from history. In a few cases posters contain sayings whose source cannot be traced but whose truths are universal.

Throughout the world there is understandable concern about children's learning. The concern takes different forms in different cultures. In some the preoccupation is with timing. At what point, if at all, in a child's learning should the provision become formal? Is 'too formal, too early' necessarily a bad thing? Should there be a place for hothousing some children? Does early formal training advantage or disadvantage? What happens to childhood in such environments? What is the place of play? Should we in the West follow the approach adopted in some other cultures, of learning through play, through freedom of movement, maybe even through early responsibility? Or are our urban, industrialized, Western societies too constraining, too benchmarked and too dangerous for such 'liberal' approaches? Does 'too formal, too early' create antagonistic attitudes to learning? If so, is this the same for boys as for girls? How might children begin to form views about themselves as learners as a result of such early experiences? What happens if, as a consequence of such views being internalized and adopted as part of oneself, they harden into attitudes, beliefs and value systems?

Learning is about more than assimilating knowledge and skills. It is about more than interacting positively in different social groupings. It is about more than loading up with content. Learning is also about finding out about one's self; about who you are and who you can become. It is about making considered choices in an uncertain world. It is about extending the horizons of possibility.

In the year after Neil Armstrong first stepped onto the moon, I arrived in secondary school. We spent our first year at secondary school in mixed-ability sets. In my second year, we were placed into sets according to ability. I was good at 'doing school' and luckily had 'chosen' good parents who helped motivate me: I got into the top set. In this top set we were at the apex of a pile held up by four other sets. Because we were good at 'whatever' and there was a faint possibility that some of us might be selected again to go 17 miles away to the Academy, we had to do Latin in addition to French. The two sets below us did French but no Latin. The set below them did art and no languages. The set below art did craft and not much else. So while I conjugated, my erstwhile mates bashed lumps of metal and planed planks of wood. We settled into our new statuses:. me, confused as to why I would want to have a conversation with a table in a language no one actually spoke; them, certain in the knowledge they had three years' worth of bird tables, coffee tables and bedside cabinets awaiting them.

Our first Latin exam was due and I discovered the value of learning posters. Out of the back pages of the *New Musical Express*, I had, some time before, sent for the Athena poster catalogue. I had ordered and duly received a poster of the Earth pictured from outer space. I stuck it up above the fireplace at the end of my bed. If I shut my eyes I can see it now. A blue and white ball coming out of the blackness. It was the last thing I saw at night before the blankets went over my head. Then the torch and the transistor came out from under the pillow and I read *Teenage Mutant Horror* while listening through the earpiece to Radio Luxemburg. Often I would wake in the morning with a searing pain. The radio would be suspended inches from the floor, held in place by 10 inches of wire attached to the earpiece which was being slowly prised from my ear. When I had removed the earpiece and come to my senses, I would see Earth looking down at me. When I had gathered myself even more I would remember the exams looming and the thought struck me, 'why not learn it from bed?' And that's what I did.

I recovered the unused wallpaper rolls from the attic, cut them into poster-size pieces using Earth as a measuring stick and wrote all the verbs on the back. Earth got turned around and on the back I drew a cross section of a Roman road which, apparently, no serious Latin scholar could do without knowing. Now in the evenings, after lights out and before '208 Radio Luxemburg – the Friendly Giant', I could do Latin by torchlight. So taken was I by my innovation, I told my mate Donald. Donald had got into the Latin class because he was frightened of what his mum would do to him if he hadn't. We both knew – he and I – he wasn't very good. So I told him what I had done and suggested he should try it. We both liked a shortcut. But he said he shared a room with his brothers and didn't think they would have it, and so the moment passed.

BRIGHT SPARKS

'Nothing really great was ever achieved without effort.'

visit the website www.alite.co.uk

BRIGHT SPARKS

'To do well in anything you need the skill and the will.'

visit the website www.alite.co.uk

BRIGHT SPARKS

'If you want to change
the world, start
by changing
your attitude.'

visit the website www.alite.co.uk

Eventually, it was exam week and the day of the Latin exam. Donald and I were walking to school and he seemed in a good mood. I pointed out that it was an exam. Exams were always a pain, so why was he so cheery? 'You'll see,' he says. 'I took your advice about putting it all down somewhere where you can see it. No problemus, meus es latinus terrificus!' he added, patting his bag. I worried, but we walked on. We got there, we sat down. Mr Fairley gave out the papers, droned an instruction, pointed to the clock, got his head down and off we went.

Question one: 'Draw a cross section of a roman road, labelling all the salient features,' 10 marks – a good start. I looked across the desks and saw Donald. Donald was unrolling the largest and brightest roll of flock wallpaper I had ever seen. He had pinned its trailing edge to the floor with an ink bottle and an old pencil case, and was peering intently at the detailed writing on the back; every now and again he raised his head, scanned the room and began to write at length. The wallpaper revision method never did catch on. Donald had forgotten that Mr Fairley was part time and finished early on Mondays. 'Beat the belt' MacDougall was not so understanding.

Visual reinforcement is, however, still part of our learning repertoire. The posters contained in this booklet are designed to enhance learning attitudes and learning techniques. With a different set of attitudes and alternative techniques, Donald may not have had to ruin his mother's DIY plans. The posters provided are to help develop 'the will and the skill'. Place them in classrooms and in corridors; in the assembly hall and in the gymnasium; in the reception area and the dining area. Draw attention to them in class lessons, in assemblies, during lunch, and when parents collect their children. Encourage pupils to make their own versions and put them up at home. Have a theme of the week and put the poster in the newsletter to parents. Encourage pupils to assimilate the messages by testing their recall of phrases and sayings.

Finally I leave you with one thought about the value and prevalence of 'immersion-learning environments'. I was taken to visit a Scottish primary school by a very forthright headteacher. She said, 'We walk our talk – we *are* an immersion-learning school. Come and see.' She took me around her wonderful school. Display was everywhere. Children were using it interactively. Framed affirmation posters were in every corridor. 'Look at this', she said and took me to the girls' toilets. She flung open every cubicle, and on the back of each door was a large poster of the times tables!

Alistair Smith, January 2001

BRIGHT SPARKS

'You have never lost until you quit trying.'

visit the website www.alite.co.uk

BRIGHT SPARKS

'You are as honest as your intentions.'

visit the website www.alite.co.uk

BRIGHT SPARKS

'There's a thin line between being a leader and being a ring leader.'

Susan Kovalik

visit the website www.alite.co.uk

BRIGHT SPARKS

'Never, never, never give up.'

Winston Churchill

visit the website www.alite.co.uk

BRIGHT SPARKS

'Stand up for what is right – even if you stand alone.'

visit the website www.alite.co.uk

BRIGHT SPARKS

'Courage is doing right when everyone around is doing wrong.'

visit the website www.alite.co.uk

BRIGHT SPARKS

'Want to be trusted? Tell the truth.'

visit the website www.alite.co.uk

BRIGHT SPARKS

'Telling a lie is like seeing a ghost – it can come back to haunt you.'

visit the website www.alite.co.uk

BRIGHT SPARKS

'Small keys open big doors.'

visit the website www.alite.co.uk

BRIGHT SPARKS

'No one can do everything but everyone can do something.'

visit the website www.alite.co.uk

BRIGHT SPARKS

'Join the go-for-it gang.'

visit the website www.alite.co.uk

BRIGHT SPARKS

'The "give-it-a-go club" meets here on weekdays.'

visit the website www.alite.co.uk

BRIGHT SPARKS

'Stickability is the super secret of success.'

visit the website www.alite.co.uk

BRIGHT SPARKS

'Nothing will work unless you do.'

visit the website www.alite.co.uk

BRIGHT SPARKS

'If it's to be, it's up to me!'

visit the website www.alite.co.uk

BRIGHT SPARKS

'The number one rule for an amazing brain is: use it or lose it.'

visit the website www.alite.co.uk

BRIGHT SPARKS

'Your belief in your ability has a profound effect on your ability.'

visit the website www.alite.co.uk

BRIGHT SPARKS

'When you believe, then you can begin to achieve.'

visit the website www.alite.co.uk

BRIGHT SPARKS

'To do well in anything you need the skill and the will.'

visit the website www.alite.co.uk

BRIGHT SPARKS

A is for Attitude

B is for Belief

C is for Courage

visit the website www.alite.co.uk

BRIGHT SPARKS

'Attitude plus aptitude equals altitude.'

visit the website www.alite.co.uk

BRIGHT SPARKS

'I like to work and I'm glad we struggled with it.'

Shaznay Lewis, All Saints

visit the website www.alite.co.uk

BRIGHT SPARKS

'Dare to dream.'

visit the website www.alite.co.uk

BRIGHT SPARKS

'We all have the ability to shape the way our lives will turn out.'

Trevor McDonald, news presenter

visit the website www.alite.co.uk

BRIGHT SPARKS

''cos I'm free'

Tattoo on the shoulder of Cathy Freeman,
Olympic 400-metres gold medallist

visit the website www.alite.co.uk

BRIGHT SPARKS

'Smiles are contagious — is yours?'

visit the website www.alite.co.uk

BRIGHT SPARKS

'Treat others as you would like to be treated yourself.'

visit the website www.alite.co.uk

BRIGHT SPARKS

'Smart people find good in everybody and interest in everything.'

visit the website www.alite.co.uk

BRIGHT SPARKS

'We all have ability. The difference is how we use it.'

Stevie Wonder, singer and songwriter

visit the website   www.alite.co.uk

BRIGHT SPARKS

'We are all equally different.'

visit the website www.alite.co.uk

BRIGHT SPARKS

Winners are:

too busy to be sad,

too positive to be doubtful,

too optimistic to be fearful,

too determined to be defeated.

BRIGHT SPARKS

d ifferent
i ndividuals
v aluing
e ach other,
r egardless of
s kin
i ntellect
t alent or
y ears

visit the website www.alite.co.uk

BRIGHT SPARKS

'Don't just think it – ink it!'

visit the website www.alite.co.uk

BRIGHT SPARKS

'There is no "I" in team.'

Tony Adams, former England football captain

visit the website www.alite.co.uk

BRIGHT SPARKS

'The enemy of learning is forgetting to relax.'

visit the website www.alite.co.uk

BRIGHT SPARKS

'You will always miss 100% of the shots that you never take.'

Wayne Gretzky, ice hockey star

BRIGHT SPARKS

'Tread softly, for you tread on my dreams.'

W.B. Yeats

BRIGHT SPARKS

'There is nothing either good or bad, but thinking makes it so.'

William Shakespeare, *Hamlet*

visit the website www.alite.co.uk

BRIGHT SPARKS

'God has given me a gift, but I have to make use of it.'

Prince Naseem Hamed, world champion boxer

visit the website www.alite.co.uk

BRIGHT SPARKS

'If you can dream it, you can do it.'

Walt Disney

visit the website www.alite.co.uk

BRIGHT SPARKS

'Every day find one thing you don't like doing and just try it.

Every day find one thing you don't think you are good at it and just practise it.

Every day find one question you haven't asked and just ask it.'

visit the website www.alite.co.uk

BRIGHT SPARKS

'Difficulties are opportunities to better things; they are stepping stones to greater experience.'

Bryan Adams, rock musician

visit the website www.alite.co.uk

BRIGHT SPARKS

'It is through education and learning that we can ultimately achieve all our goals and desires.'

Colin Jackson, world-record hurdler

visit the website www.alite.co.uk

BRIGHT SPARKS

'The future belongs to those who believe in the beauty of their dreams.'

Eleanor Roosevelt

BRIGHT SPARKS

'Always remember that your own resolution to succeed is more important than anything else.'

Abraham Lincoln, former President of the USA

BRIGHT SPARKS

'Education means never having the feeling of inadequacy in normal everyday life.'

Duncan Goodhew, Olympic swimming gold medallist

visit the website www.alite.co.uk

BRIGHT SPARKS

'Macho does not prove mucho.'

Zsa Zsa Gabor, actress

visit the website www.alite.co.uk

BRIGHT SPARKS

'Imaginative thinkers will be the ones working in the 21st century.'

Griff Rhys Jones, broadcaster

visit the website www.alite.co.uk

BRIGHT SPARKS

'No one ever got better by always getting it right.'

visit the website www.alite.co.uk

BRIGHT SPARKS

'Imagination is more important than knowledge.'

Albert Einstein

visit the website www.alite.co.uk

BRIGHT SPARKS

'If it's not going to matter in five years it doesn't matter now.'

Cher, singer and actress

visit the website www.alite.co.uk

BRIGHT SPARKS

'Tens of thousands of people never find out where their talent is. Where else are they going to find out but at school?'

Terry Pratchett, author

visit the website www.alite.co.uk

BRIGHT SPARKS

'Genius is one per cent inspiration, ninety-nine per cent perspiration.'

Thomas Alva Edison, American inventor

visit the website www.alite.co.uk

BRIGHT SPARKS

'Never tell me the odds!'

Han Solo, *Star Wars*

visit the website www.alite.co.uk

BRIGHT SPARKS

'Dream as if you'll live forever. Live as if you'll die tomorrow.'

James Dean, film star

visit the website www.alite.co.uk

BRIGHT SPARKS

'Education can open doors and the more doors open to you the more chance you have in life.'

Sharron Davies, MBE, Olympic silver medallist and television sports presenter

BRIGHT SPARKS

'It's how you deal with failure that determines how you achieve success.'

David Feherty, professional golfer

BRIGHT SPARKS

'Imagination is the highest kite you can fly.'

Lauren Bacall, Hollywood actress

BRIGHT SPARKS

'Whether you think you can, or whether you think you can't – you're probably right.'

Henry Ford, industrialist and car maker

BRIGHT SPARKS

'One of the things I learned when I was negotiating was that until I changed in myself I could not change others.'

Nelson Mandela, world statesman

BRIGHT SPARKS

'Too hot,
too cold,
too still,
too thirsty,
too hungry
and
you won't learn
much.'

visit the website www.alite.co.uk

BRIGHT SPARKS

'Don't be a fool – reading is cool.'

visit the website www.alite.co.uk

BRIGHT SPARKS

'Succeed – Read!'

visit the website www.alite.co.uk

BRIGHT SPARKS

'Tell me what you learned today?'

The question Albert Einstein's mother asked him when he came home from school

visit the website www.alite.co.uk

BRIGHT SPARKS

Brain food
fish
rice
cereal
pasta
chicken
vegetables
fruit
milk

Strain food
sugary stuff
pop
crisps
chips
cakes
stuff with artificial colours
sweets

visit the website   www.alite.co.uk

BRIGHT SPARKS

'For studying, a little and often is best.'

visit the website www.alite.co.uk

BRIGHT SPARKS

'Before you start, ask yourself: what do I already know about this?'

visit the website www.alite.co.uk

BRIGHT SPARKS

'There is no failure, only feedback.'

visit the website www.alite.co.uk

BRIGHT SPARKS

'Getting stuck is
OK,
staying stuck is not
– good learners
practise
at
getting unstuck.'

visit the website www.alite.co.uk

BRIGHT SPARKS

When you get stuck, you get unstuck by...

- going over the problem again, carefully, to see where you might have made a mistake...

- pretending you are a teacher and giving yourself some advice on how to do it better...

- using a learning tool – like a dictionary or a thesaurus or a reference book...

- asking an expert for help!

BRIGHT SPARKS

Good advice for working at home:

1. find a quiet place with space...
2. gather everything you need...
3. think about what you are going to do...
4. do it...
5. test that you know it...
6. give yourself a reward for doing it.

BRIGHT SPARKS

Good advice for remembering important facts:

1. draw a poster of the important facts...
2. describe all the important facts in a quiet voice to yourself...
3. try to teach someone else or imagine teaching someone else the important facts...
4. act out the important facts...
5. test yourself.

BRIGHT SPARKS

Put on your memory specs:

s ee it

p ersonalize it

e xaggerate it

c onnect it

s hare it

visit the website   www.alite.co.uk

BRIGHT SPARKS

Two secrets of memory:

1. remember what it looked like;

2. remember where it was.

BRIGHT SPARKS

'Put up learning posters and keywords on your bedroom wall, lie on the bed, shut your eyes, describe them in words, test yourself — and be amazed.'

visit the website www.alite.co.uk

BRIGHT SPARKS

'Test yourself!'

visit the website www.alite.co.uk

BRIGHT SPARKS

GOALS –

g o
o ut
a nd
l earn
s omething

visit the website www.alite.co.uk

BRIGHT SPARKS

'The ability to set goals and work towards them marks the difference between success and failure.'

visit the website www.alite.co.uk

BRIGHT SPARKS

'Put your target card on your desk to remind you to go for it.'

visit the website www.alite.co.uk

BRIGHT SPARKS

'Write out your goal, then the steps to get there, then start your journey.'

visit the website www.alite.co.uk

BRIGHT SPARKS

'The best question is the one you are about to ask...'

visit the website www.alite.co.uk

BRIGHT SPARKS

'Good learners ask good questions…

…and good questions start in your head.'

visit the website www.alite.co.uk

BRIGHT SPARKS

'You learn
best by
seeing it,
hearing about it
and
doing it
for yourself.'

visit the website www.alite.co.uk

Both hands in a fist...

Remember a time when you did something you enjoyed and did it really well...

see yourself doing it, listen to the sounds and feel how good it was...

do this again 'til you begin to feel warm in your tummy

now squeeze both hands in a fist.

Do this again – remember doing something really well, see yourself doing it, hear the sounds, feel the warmth in your tummy; now squeeze both hands in a fist...

So, if you are really worried about doing something: remember doing well, feel the warmth, squeeze both hands in a fist...

and then be successful!

BRIGHT SPARKS

To do magic spelling...

First, remember what it felt like when you did really well last time...

then, look at the proper spelling of the word...

now shut your eyes and,

see the word and spell it aloud quietly to yourself as you write it with your finger in front of your face.

Practise again...

and again...

now test yourself.

BRIGHT SPARKS

Train for magic spelling...

First, remember what it felt like
when you did really well last time.

Then imagine a train with little carriages...

then, look at the proper spelling of
the word...

now shut your eyes and...

see each letter of the word written
on the carriages of your train.

With your eyes shut, watch the train
and read out the letters.

visit the website www.alite.co.uk

BRIGHT SPARKS

Catch the train to spell really well...

Remember doing good spelling.

Imagine your train, shut your eyes and...

see the letters of the word on the carriages of your train.

Keep your eyes shut and imagine pulling your train in front of your face.

As you pull from right to left, see the letters on each carriage...

read them aloud, then park your train.

visit the website www.alite.co.uk

BRIGHT SPARKS

Do the sum hum...

Put your hand on your tummy and remember what it felt like the last time you did sums really well.

Now think of a song you really like and hum the song quietly to yourself.

Now find an easy sum to practise.

As you do the sum, hum the song.

Now try a harder sum and hum the song.

Now try telling yourself what to do to the tune of the song.

visit the website   www.alite.co.uk

BRIGHT SPARKS

As you do it – talk yourself through it...

Pretend you are the best maths teacher in the whole world and...

when you do maths talk yourself through the workings as you go.

Make sure you talk yourself through all of it.

When you get really good, practise doing the talking in your head!

visit the website www.alite.co.uk

BRIGHT SPARKS

'Trying to remember important things without going over them again, is like trying to fill the bath without putting the plug in.'

visit the website www.alite.co.uk

BRIGHT SPARKS

'Within 45 seconds of standing up there is 15% more oxygen in your brain!'

visit the website www.alite.co.uk

BRIGHT SPARKS

'Each one teach one to show you know.'

visit the website www.alite.co.uk

BRIGHT SPARKS

'You learn 10% of what you read, 15% of what you hear, but 80% of what you do for yourself.'

visit the website www.alite.co.uk

BRIGHT SPARKS

'The hidden secret of study success is to learn to test yourself until you get better.'

visit the website www.alite.co.uk

BRIGHT SPARKS

'When you're stressed, you're stuffed – I practise every shot in my head until I know I can do it.'

Colin Montgomerie, professional golfer

BRIGHT SPARKS

'The first place to practise being successful is in your head.'

visit the website www.alite.co.uk

BRIGHT SPARKS

'You can have it all – you just can't have it all at one time.'

visit the website www.alite.co.uk

BRIGHT SPARKS

Practise exam technique in your head – imagine you...

1. sit down, make yourself comfortable and look around...
2. breathe deeply and relax...
3. open the exam paper and flick through, a page at a time, to the end, then breathe deeply...
4. read the questions and look at the marks for each...
5. write down the time to spend on each question alongside it...
6. map a quick answer with keywords for each question and...
7. successfully answer all the questions – and pass the exam!

visit the website www.alite.co.uk

BRIGHT SPARKS

10 suggestions for schools using these posters

1. Display above eye level in classrooms and around the school.
2. Display in classrooms, in a designated space, as a theme for the week.
3. Use as a teaching tool for discussion, for example asking children to choose their favourite saying and explaining why it is important to them.
4. Encourage children to copy the posters and stick them up at home.
5. Use as screen savers on the school computer network.
6. Put into pupil planners and homework diaries.
7. Use as a theme for an assembly or for a series of 'learning to learn' assemblies.
8. Put onto the school website.
9. Put into the parent newsletter and explain how they can be used at home.
10. Use as a staff development tool. Include posters in staffrooms and encourage staff to explore ways of using the posters with pupils and developing the theme throughout their teaching.

visit the website   www.alite.co.uk

BRIGHT SPARKS

Acknowledgements

Quote by *Susan Kovalik*. By permission of Debora Schweikl.

Quote by Sir Winston S. Churchill. Reproduced with permission of Curtis Brown Ltd, London, on behalf of the Estate of Sir Winston S. Churchill. Copyright Winston S. Churchill 1948.

Quote from Sir Trevor McDonald. Reproduced by permission of ITN Press Office and Sir Trevor McDonald.

Quote from Catherine Freeman. Reproduced by permission of Catherine Freeman and IMG Australia.

Quote by W.B. Yeats, from *He wishes for the Cloths of Heaven*. Reproduced by permission of A P Watt on behalf of Michael B. Yeats.

Quote *If you can dream it, you can do it* (Walt Disney).

Quote from Bryan Adams. Reproduced by permission of Bryan Adams.

Quote by Colin Jackson. Reproduced by permission of James Hunt MTC.

Quote by Griff Rhys Jones. Reproduced by permission of Griff Rhys Jones and Talkback Agency.

Quote by Sharron Davies. Reproduced by permission of Sharron Davies, MBE, Olympic silver medallist and sports presenter.

Quote by Henry Ford. Reproduced by permission of Mark A. Greene, Henry Ford Museum and Greenfield Village.

Quote by Colin Montgomerie. Reproduced by permission of Colin Montgomerie – seven times Winner of the European Tour Order of Merit

Quote by Prince Naseem Hamed. Reproduced by permission of Riath Hamed.

Quote by Duncan Goodhew. Reproduced by permission of Duncan Goodhew.

visit the website   www.alite.co.uk

Excellence in Word Problems

Year 2

Jane Bovey and
Jo Waterman

RISING★STARS

Rising Stars UK Ltd, 76 Farnaby Road, Bromley BR1 4BH

www.risingstars-uk.com

Every effort has been made to trace copyright holders and obtain their permission for the use of copyright materials. The authors and publisher will gladly receive information enabling them to rectify any error or omission in subsequent editions.

All facts are correct at time of going to press.

Published 2004
Text, design and layout © Rising Stars UK Ltd.

Editorial Consultants: Dominique Turner and Frances Ridley
Design: Clive Sutherland
Illustrations: Louisa Burville-Riley (children and teacher characters)
Cover photo: Alamy
Cover Design: Burville-Riley

All rights reserved. No part of this publication may be reproduced, stored in a retrieval system, or transmitted, in any form by any means, electronic, mechanical, photocopying, recording or otherwise, without the prior permission of Rising Stars.

British Library Cataloguing in Publication Data.
A CIP record for this book is available from the British Library.

ISBN: 1-904591-64-7

Printed by The Cromwell Press, Trowbridge, Wiltshire

Contents

How to use this book	4
Using Excellence	5
Objectives	6
Ten top tips for problem solving	8
Ten top tips for handling homework	9
Copymasters 1 – 31	10
Resource copymasters 1 – 4	41
Answers	45

How to use this book

Excellence in Word Problems Year 2 is a series of copymasters designed to support teaching and learning of the Problem Solving Objectives within the National Numeracy Strategy.

It is part of the *Excellence* series of products that support learning across the Primary Numeracy Curriculum and includes books on Calculations, Word Problems and Fractions, Decimals and Percentages.

How each copymaster works:

Main activity
Each main activity covers a specific objective, indicated on pages 6–7, and covers the main topics within the Solving Problems strand of the NNS: making decisions, reasoning and solving problems in context.
Children are invited to record their answers in a variety of ways.

Challenge!
All activity copymasters end with a Challenge, which extends the child's learning and provides an opportunity for more able children to develop their understanding of the concept. Children often need to record their answers on the back of the copymaster or on a separate sheet.

Resource Copymasters
In addition to the activity copymasters, there is a range of four Resource copymasters providing most of the resources required to deliver the activities, which means that the book is completely self-contained.

Heading and Introduction
These provide some basic information on the concept covered in the copymaster and can be used by the teaching assistant, parent or carer to support the child's work.

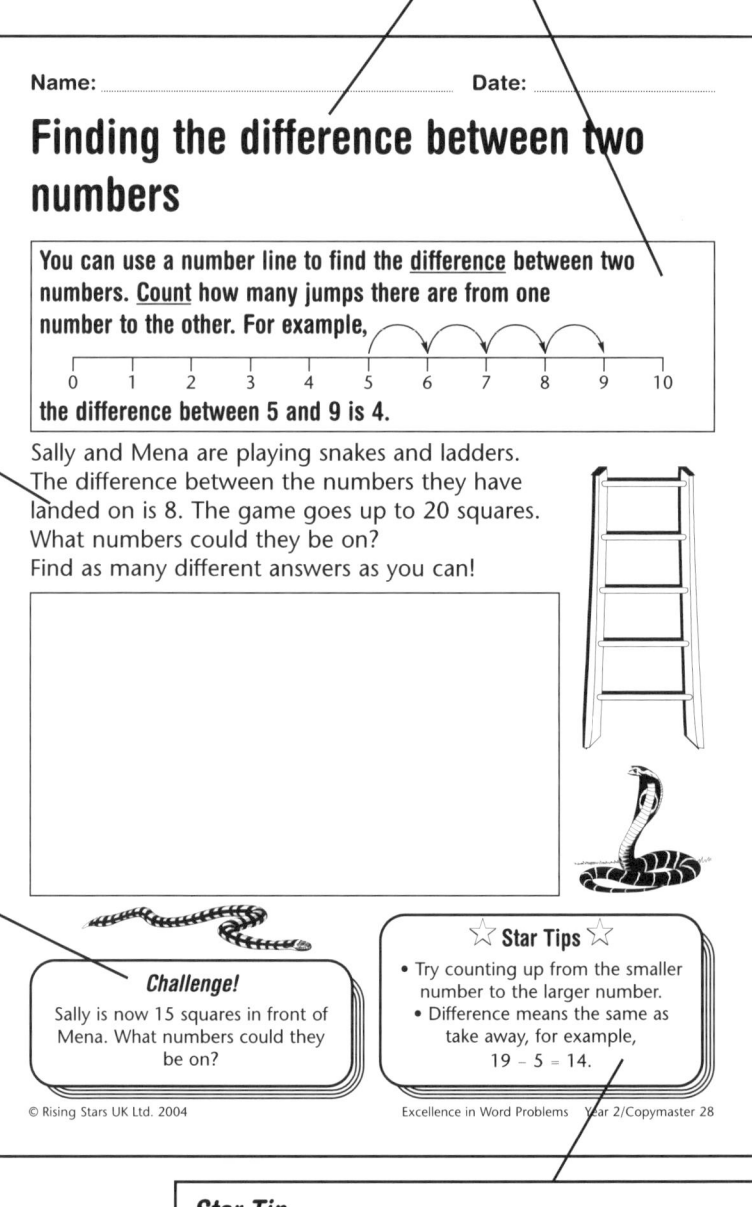

Name: _____ Date: _____

Finding the difference between two numbers

You can use a number line to find the <u>difference</u> between two numbers. <u>Count</u> how many jumps there are from one number to the other. For example,

the difference between 5 and 9 is 4.

Sally and Mena are playing snakes and ladders. The difference between the numbers they have landed on is 8. The game goes up to 20 squares. What numbers could they be on?
Find as many different answers as you can!

Challenge!
Sally is now 15 squares in front of Mena. What numbers could they be on?

☆ Star Tips ☆
• Try counting up from the smaller number to the larger number.
• Difference means the same as take away, for example, 19 − 5 = 14.

© Rising Stars UK Ltd. 2004   Excellence in Word Problems Year 2/Copymaster 28

Star Tip
Star Tips support children and those assisting them by providing clues or strategies for solving the problems on each page.

Using Excellence

In the classroom

Excellence in Word Problems provides a perfect resource bank for whole class and individual work. Putting each copymaster onto an OHP allows the teacher to ask children to offer their own methods for solving each problem, and to explain the concept by doing the first part of the question.

Excellence in Word Problems can also be used in individual and paired work, especially to encourage children to share their problem solving strategies and talk about how they made decisions.

Out of class and for homework

Each of the activities are short and focused. They can be used at the end of a topic to assess and extend the application of the skills covered. The Challenges are most useful here.

Because the activities are set within a variety of contexts and require few, if any, resources, they are perfect for photocopying and sending home.

Tips

We have included a further two copymasters to support parents if you choose to use this book as the basis for your numeracy homework:

- *Ten top tips for problem solving* (page 8) provides children and their parents with the tools required to answer all the questions. The copymaster provides them with strategies, a framework for answering problems and key issues to watch out for.
- *Ten top tips for handling homework* (page 9) is a copymaster that gives parents advice and support to make homework a regular and successful part of their child's schooling.

Objectives

Copymaster	Title	National Numeracy Strategy Objective
1	Odd and even numbers	Recognise odd and even numbers to 20.
2	Number sequences	Count on in steps of 2, 3, 4, 5 and more.
3	Partitioning two-digit numbers	Know what each digit in a two-digit number represents.
4	Ordering numbers	Order numbers in 'real life' contexts.
5	Estimating	Make estimates of numbers and measurements in a range of practical contexts.
6	Rounding numbers	Begin to round numbers less than 100 to the nearest ten.
7	Fractions of shapes	Recognise $\frac{1}{2}$ and $\frac{1}{4}$ as one half and one quarter.
8	Fractions of numbers	Recognise $\frac{1}{2}$ and $\frac{1}{4}$ as one half and one quarter.
9	Addition	Understand that more than two numbers can be added together.
10	Addition and subtraction	Understand addition and subtraction.
11	Multiplication and division	Use simple multiplication and division to solve 'story problems' about numbers in 'real life'.
12	Division	Understand the operation of division as sharing equally.
13	Checking your answers	Check results of calculations using various methods.
14	Showing your working out	Explain and record how a problem was solved.
15	Missing numbers, missing signs	Choose and use appropriate number operations to solve problems.
16	Problem solving	Use mental addition/subtraction to solve story problems about numbers in 'real life' contexts.

Copymaster	Title	National Numeracy Strategy Objective
17	Solving number puzzles	Solve puzzles and problems in a variety of contexts.
18	Solving shape puzzles	Solve puzzles and problems in a variety of contexts.
19	Totals of coins	Find totals and give change.
20	Finding totals of coins	Use mental addition and subtraction to solve money problems.
21	Time problems	Use mental calculation strategies to solve measurement problems set in a variety of contexts.
22	Length problems	Use mental calculation strategies to solve measurement problems set in a variety of contexts.
23	Symmetrical patterns	Begin to recognise and sketch a line of symmetry.
24	Making 3-D shapes	Describe 3-D shapes and their features.
25	Venn diagrams	Classify numbers and organise them in lists and simple tables.
26	Presenting information	Make a simple bar chart and pictogram where the symbol represents one unit.
27	Ordinal numbers	Use and begin to read the vocabulary of comparing and ordering numbers, including ordinal numbers.
28	Finding the difference between two numbers	Understand the operation of subtraction as difference.
29	Doubling and halving	Understand doubling and halving.
30	Two step operations	Solve simple problems using more than one step.
31	Measuring capacity	Solve simple problems set in a variety of contexts.

Ten top tips for problem solving

☆ Star Tip 1 ☆
Read each question *carefully* and work out what you are being asked to do.

☆ Star Tip 2 ☆
Look carefully at the numbers or shapes you are going to be working with.

☆ Star Tip 3 ☆
Do your calculations carefully and *check the answer*.

☆ Star Tip 4 ☆
Always *show your working*, or 'method'. This will help you to keep track of what you have done.

☆ Star Tip 5 ☆
Always *include your units* of measurement (grams, litres, cm) in the answer.

☆ Star Tip 6 ☆
When you first read through a question *underline important words and numbers*. This will help you to remember the important bits!

☆ Star Tip 7 ☆
Draw a picture to help you. Sometimes a question is easier if you can 'see' it. Drawing six apples may help you if you need to divide them!

☆ Star Tip 8 ☆
If the problem has a number of steps, break it down and do *one step at a time*.

☆ Star Tip 9 ☆
Sometimes an answer will 'sound right'. Read it out (quietly) and listen. *Does it make sense?*

☆ Star Tip 10 ☆
Always remember: read the question and then read it again.

© Rising Stars UK Ltd. 2004

You may photocopy this page

Ten top tips for handling homework

⭐ **Star Tip 1** ⭐

Show an interest in your child's homework. This essential input will underline its importance.

⭐ **Star Tip 2** ⭐

Try to find a time each week when homework is always done. This will begin good habits that will support your child throughout his or her schooling.

⭐ **Star Tip 3** ⭐

Find somewhere for your child to do the homework. It should be light, quiet and undisturbed by other members of the family.

⭐ **Star Tip 4** ⭐

Make sure your child has everything he or she needs for the homework; pencils, an eraser and paper are usually all that is required.

⭐ **Star Tip 5** ⭐

Don't let homework become 'hardwork'. If you and your child are struggling to get the homework done, leave it for a time and come back when you are both feeling better about it.

⭐ **Star Tip 6** ⭐

Encourage and support but never actually do your child's homework. Though it might feel like you are helping, your child may use this as a way to avoid doing the work.

⭐ **Star Tip 7** ⭐

If you feel the homework is too hard or too easy, speak to your child's teacher. He or she will be able to reassure you.

⭐ **Star Tip 8** ⭐

If your school asks for comments, try to give them as often as possible. By working in partnership with your child's teacher, everyone will succeed.

⭐ **Star Tip 9** ⭐

Always praise your child for their hard work, even if they found homework difficult. Praise from you will mean a lot and will boost your child's confidence.

⭐ **Star Tip 10** ⭐

Encourage your child to 'read the question and then read it again' every time.

© Rising Stars UK Ltd. 2004

Name: _____   Date: _____

Odd and even numbers

Numbers are always either <u>odd</u> or <u>even</u>. Some odd numbers are 1, 3, 5 and 7. Some even numbers are 2, 4, 6 and 8.

1 Can you find out what happens when two *identical* odd numbers are added together? Make three more number sentences here.
For example, 1 + 1 = 2

☐ + ☐ = ☐   ☐ + ☐ = ☐   ☐ + ☐ = ☐

2 Now make three more sums by adding two *different* odd numbers together. Can you see a pattern?
For example, 1 + 3 = 4

☐ + ☐ = ☐   ☐ + ☐ = ☐   ☐ + ☐ = ☐

3 Try adding two *identical* even numbers together. Make another three sums here.
For example, 2 + 2 = 4

☐ + ☐ = ☐   ☐ + ☐ = ☐   ☐ + ☐ = ☐

4 Now make three more sums by adding two *different* even numbers together. Can you see another pattern?
For example, 4 + 2 = 6

☐ + ☐ = ☐   ☐ + ☐ = ☐   ☐ + ☐ = ☐

Challenge!
What happens if you add an even and an odd number together?

☆ **Star Tips** ☆
• Even numbers can be split into two equal groups.
• With odd numbers there will be one left over.

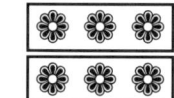

8   7

© Rising Stars UK Ltd. 2004   Excellence in Word Problems   Year 2/Copymaster 1

Name: .... Date: ....

Number sequences

A number sequence is a <u>pattern</u> of numbers. A sequence always follows a <u>rule</u>. For example, 5, 10, 15, 20… the rule is counting in fives.

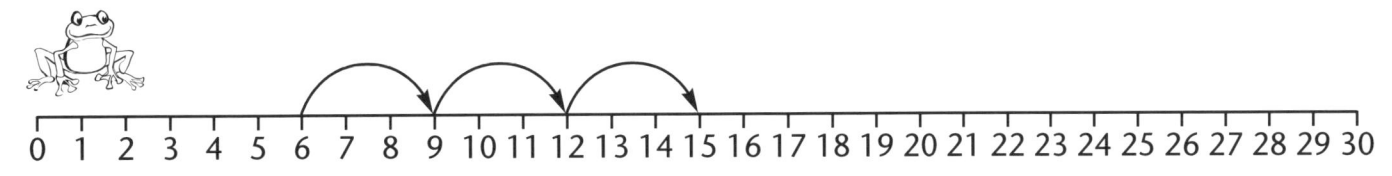

0 5 10 15 20

0 1 2 3 4 5 6 7 8 9 10 11 12 13 14 15 16 17 18 19 20 21 22 23 24 25 26 27 28 29 30

1 A frog is jumping along a number line. He lands on numbers 6, 9, 12 and 15. What other numbers will he land on? Can you describe the pattern?

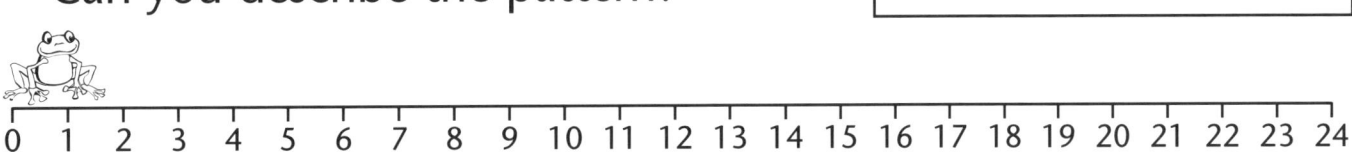

0 1 2 3 4 5 6 7 8 9 10 11 12 13 14 15 16 17 18 19 20 21 22 23 24

2 Another frog is ready to jump. He wants his jumps to include numbers 4 and 20. Write a number sequence to show what other numbers he will jump on.

0 1 2 3 4 5 6 7 8 9 10 11 12 13 14 15 16 17 18 19 20 21 22 23 24 25 26 27 28 29 30

3 The last frog is jumping backwards! He started on number 30 and finished on number 10. What other numbers do you think he landed on?

Challenge!
A number sequence in steps of 2 from 0 shows the multiples of 2. A sequence in steps of 5 from 0 shows the multiples of 5. Can you find numbers that are multiples of 2 and 5?

☆ Star Tips ☆
- Draw a number line to help you.
- Make sure all of the jumps are the same size.

© Rising Stars UK Ltd. 2004   Excellence in Word Problems   Year 2/Copymaster 2

Name: ....   Date: ....

Partitioning two-digit numbers

A two-digit number is made up of <u>tens</u> and <u>units</u>.
13 = 10 + 3 or *1* ten and *3* units.

1 The Maths Magician is sorting out his numbers and needs your help! Write five numbers that will fit in each group.

  a Numbers with 5 tens ☐ ☐ ☐ ☐ ☐

  b Numbers with 3 units ☐ ☐ ☐ ☐ ☐

  c Numbers with 0 units ☐ ☐ ☐ ☐ ☐

  d Numbers with 1 ten ☐ ☐ ☐ ☐ ☐

  e Even numbers with 4 tens ☐ ☐ ☐ ☐ ☐

2 Can you fill in the missing numbers?

  a 37 = 30 + ☐   **b** 28 = ☐ + 8   **c** 96 = ☐ + ☐

Challenge!
Well done! Now the Maths Magician needs help sorting his three-digit numbers. Write down four sentences for each of these questions.
1 Numbers with 2 hundreds and 3 tens.
2 Numbers with 4 hundreds and 5 units.
3 Numbers with 9 hundreds and 1 ten.

☆ Star Tip ☆
• Use a hundred square to help you.
• Remember:
H   T   U
1   3   7
is one hundred and thirty seven.

© Rising Stars UK Ltd. 2004   Excellence in Word Problems   Year 2/Copymaster 3

Name: .... **Date:** ....

Ordering numbers

Numbers can be <u>ordered</u> from smallest to largest or largest to smallest.

These numbers have fallen off the scoring board at an ice-skating competition.

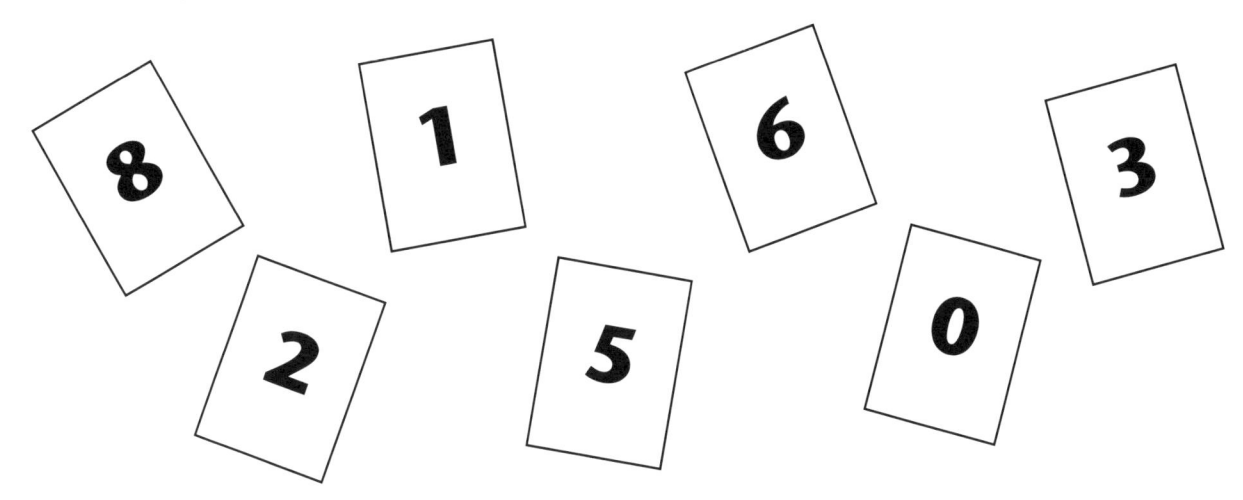

8 1 6 3
2 5 0

1 Can you make a two-digit number by using two of the cards? Write it in the box. Make three more two-digit numbers in this way. Write them all in order from largest to smallest.

2 Now try making four different two-digit numbers. Number them from smallest to largest.

Challenge!
Use the digits 7, 9 and 4 to make six different three-digit numbers. Then write them in order from smallest to largest.

☆ Star Tip ☆
To order your numbers, first look at the hundreds, then tens and then the units.

© Rising Stars UK Ltd. 2004 Excellence in Word Problems Year 2/Copymaster 4

Name: .... Date: ....

Estimating

An estimate is a <u>sensible guess</u>! You can estimate an answer before you work it out. This will help you make sure your answer is right.

It is Sports Day, and some children are doing the long jump.
Can you estimate how far each of these children have jumped?

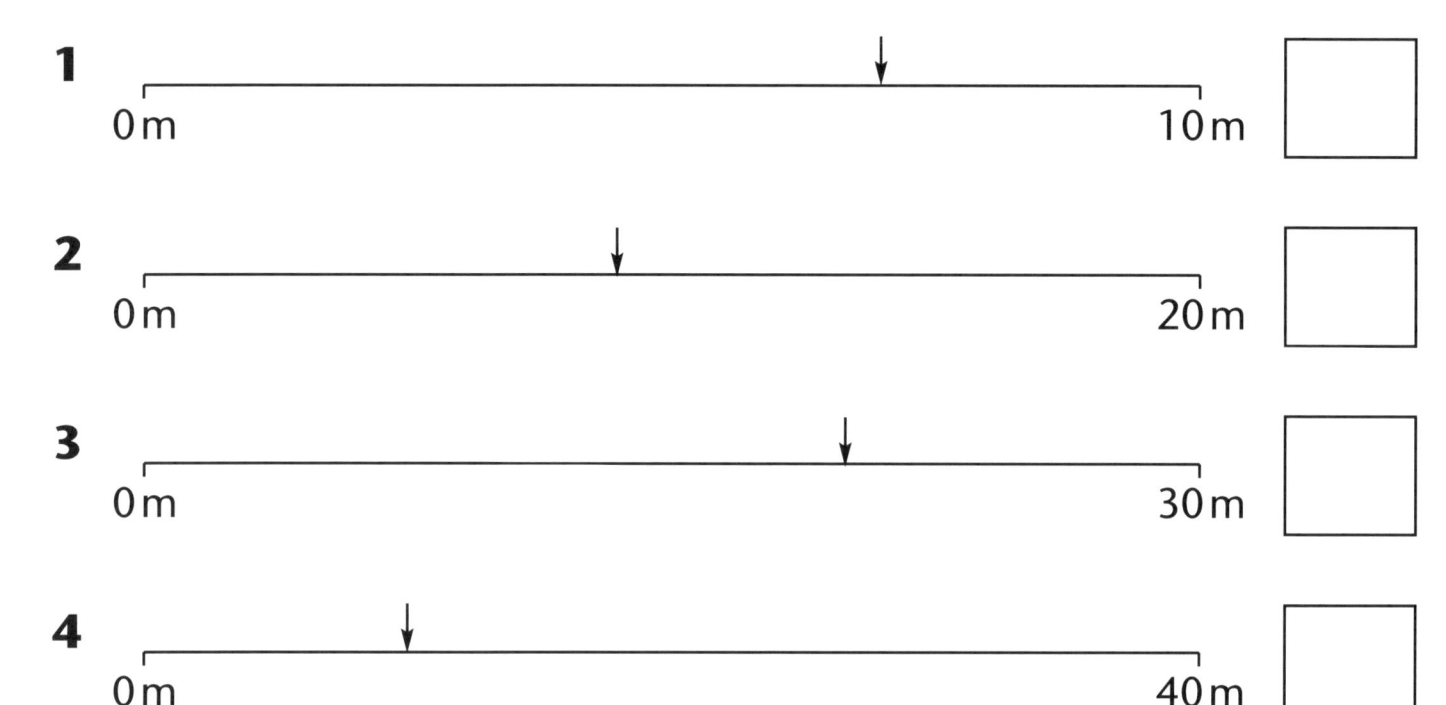

1   ├─────────────────────↓────────┤   ☐
    0 m   10 m

2   ├─────────────↓──────────────┤   ☐
    0 m   20 m

3   ├──────────────────↓─────────┤   ☐
    0 m   30 m

4   ├────↓───────────────────────┤   ☐
    0 m   40 m

Challenge!
Draw your own long jumps to show these estimations, or use this number line to mark how far they jumped.
- Lucy jumped 10 m
- Tim jumped 13 m
- Sharny jumped 25 m
- Dapali jumped 18 m

├──────────────────────────────┤
0 m   30 m

☆ Star Tips ☆
- Start by finding the middle number on the line.
- Is the long jump greater or smaller than the middle?
- Check to make sure you **estimate** is **sensible**.

Gold

© Rising Stars UK Ltd. 2004   Excellence in Word Problems   Year 2/Copymaster 5

Rounding numbers

Sometimes numbers are <u>rounded</u> to the <u>nearest</u> ten. 57 can be rounded to 60, as it is nearer to 60 than to 50.

A shopkeeper is not very good at giving change so he wants to round his prices to the nearest ten. Can you work out what the new prices of each item will be?

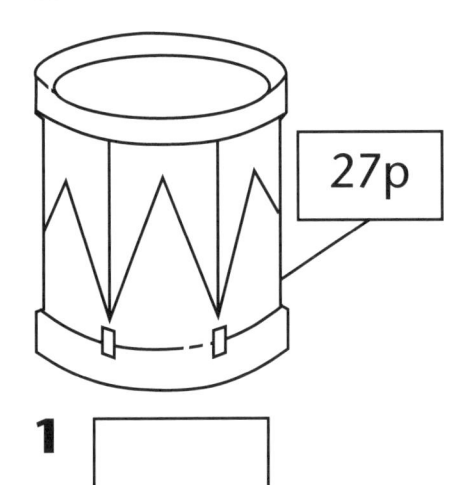

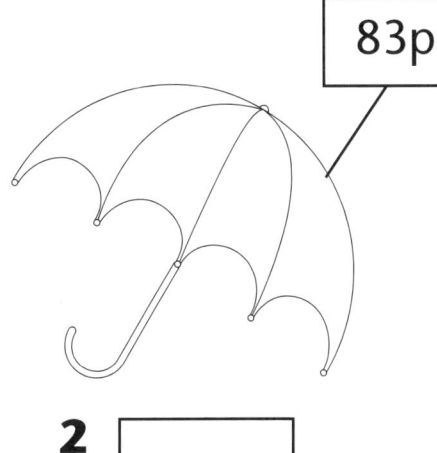

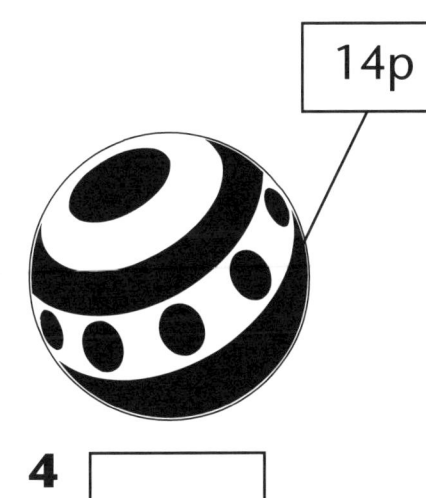

1. 27p

2. 83p

3. 76p

4. 14p

5. 31p

6. 59p

Challenge!
Can you write three **even** numbers and three **odd** numbers that could be rounded to these numbers?
a) 40   b) 60   c) 80   d) 100

☆ Star Tip ☆
When rounding a number with five units, you always **round up** to the nearest ten, so, 75 would be rounded to 80.

Name: ....   Date: ....

Fractions of shapes

When shapes are divided into equal parts, each part is called a 'fraction' of the whole shape. For example:

Half, or $\frac{1}{2}$, of this circle is coloured in.

One third, or $\frac{1}{3}$, of this rectangle is coloured in.

One quarter, or $\frac{1}{4}$, of this square is coloured in.

You have entered a competition to design a new flag. Each flag must be divided into quarters ($\frac{1}{4}$).

Use two colours to decorate your flags. How many different flags can you make?

Challenge!
Congratulations! You are through to the next round. Now, divide the flags into thirds ($\frac{1}{3}$) and colour them using three colours.

☆Star Tips☆
- Make sure all the parts are equal.
- Remember to use a ruler to draw straight lines.

© Rising Stars UK Ltd. 2004   Excellence in Word Problems   Year 2/Copymaster 7

Name: .... Date: ....

Fractions of numbers

Numbers can be <u>divided</u> into equal parts.
Each part is called a '<u>fraction</u>' of the whole number.
Half, or $\frac{1}{2}$, of these cows are black. Half of 6 is 3.

Answer these questions and draw pictures to help you.

1 Farmer Fred has 10 animals on his farm. Half of his animals are pigs. He has 3 cows and the rest are sheep. How many sheep and pigs are there?

2 There are 8 smarties on a plate. Half of them are green, one quarter are red. The rest are orange. How many are there of each colour?

3 Class 2W are making a fruit salad with 12 pieces of fruit. One quarter are grapes, one quarter are cherries and rest are strawberries. How many are there of each fruit?

Challenge!
Class 2B has 20 children. 10 of them have blue eyes, 5 have green eyes and the rest have brown eyes. Can you write these as fractions?

☆ Star Tips ☆
• When we write fractions, the biggest number goes at the bottom.
• To find a quarter, find half then halve it again.

© Rising Stars UK Ltd. 2004   Excellence in Word Problems   Year 2/Copymaster 8

Name: .... Date: ....

Addition

Addition means finding the total when two or more numbers are added together. You can also use the words <u>sum of</u>, <u>plus</u>, and <u>altogether</u>.

| 9 | 3 | 6 | 5 | 1 |

1 Use the numbers above to write ten addition calculations.

2 a Now use the numbers at the top of the page to find five different two-digit numbers to add together.
   b What is the largest total you can make?

Challenge!
Using the numbers 9, 3, 6, 5 and 1, make eight three-digit numbers and add them together.

☆ Star Tip ☆
Always start with the largest number first.

© Rising Stars UK Ltd. 2004   Excellence in Word Problems   Year 2/Copymaster 9

Name: ....   Date: ....

Addition and subtraction

Addition means finding the total when two numbers are added together. Subtraction means finding the total left over when a smaller number is taken away from a larger one.

1 Miss Green has written some calculations on the board using invisible ink. Can you work out what the missing numbers could be?

a ☐ + ☐ = 18

b ☐ − ☐ = 12

c ☐ + ☐ = 19

d ☐ − 5 = ☐

e 17 + ☐ = ☐

f 12 − ☐ = ☐

2 Now use the back of this sheet to write out three more ways to complete each problem.

Challenge!
Now try these.

☐ + ☐ + ☐ = 12

☐ + ☐ − ☐ = 9

☐ − ☐ − ☐ = 15

☐ − ☐ + ☐ = 8

☆ Star Tip ☆
Check your calculation every time to make sure your sum is correct.

© Rising Stars UK Ltd. 2004   Excellence in Word Problems   Year 2/Copymaster 10

Name: .... Date: ....

Multiplication and division

Use what you know about <u>repeated addition</u> (multiplication) and <u>sharing</u> (division) to answer these word problems.

1 One morning on the moon, an astronaut meets some aliens with 2 heads. If he can see 6 heads, how many aliens has he met?

2 Later on the astronaut meets some other aliens and they each have 5 heads. If he can see 15 heads, how many aliens are there?

3 After dinner, the astronaut and all the aliens play hide and seek together. Now the astronaut can see 18 heads behind his spaceship.
How many of each alien could be there?
How many answers can you find?

Challenge!

Some new aliens with 3 heads have joined the game. Now the astronaut can see 23 heads. What aliens could he see? Find as many answers as you can.

☆ Star Tips ☆

- Draw pictures of the aliens to help you.
- Try lots of different ways until you find an answer. There may be more than one way to do it!

© Rising Stars UK Ltd. 2004   Excellence in Word Problems   Year 2/Copymaster 11

Name: ....   Date: ....

Division

One way to divide a number is by <u>sharing</u> it into <u>equal groups</u>.

In Class 2E there are 24 children.

1 For PE Class 2E need to work in pairs.
How many pairs of children are there?

2 In an art lesson, Miss White wants the children of 2E to work in groups of 3. How many groups will there be?

3 At lunchtime there are 4 children from 2E on each table. How many tables are needed?

Challenge!
1 How many more children are needed in the class to make equal groups of 5?
2 How many more are needed to make equal groups of 10?

☆ Star Tips ☆
- Drawing pictures of the children or using cubes will help you divide the numbers.
- Make sure all the groups are equal.

© Rising Stars UK Ltd. 2004   Excellence in Word Problems   Year 2/Copymaster 12

Name: .... Date: ....

Checking your answers

When you have done a calculation you should always do it again to check your first answer is correct.

Mrs Brown has gone on holiday and wants you to mark her work.
If the calculation is correct then give it a tick. ✓
If it is wrong, give it a cross. ✗
Then write in the correct answer.

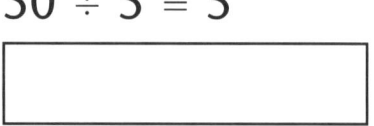

1 12 + 15 = 19 ☐

2 36 − 19 = 17 ☐

3 5 × 4 = 21 ☐

4 16 ÷ 2 = 9 ☐

5 7 × 10 = 70 ☐

6 57 + 26 = 82 ☐

7 50 ÷ 5 = 5 ☐

8 47 − 15 = 32 ☐

Challenge!
Mark these answers and write in the correct answer if you need to.
1. Sam is 12 years old. Jack is 8 years older. How old is Jack? 19
2. There were 5 sheep in each pen. How many pens are needed for 35 sheep? 7
3. Greta had 40 marbles. She gave 12 to her brother and 5 to her friend. How many did she have left? 28
4. There are 7 days in a week. How many days in 4 weeks? 103

☆ Star Tip ☆
There is always more than one way to solve the problem but only one correct answer!

© Rising Stars UK Ltd. 2004   Excellence in Word Problems   Year 2/Copymaster 13

Showing your working out

Sometimes it is important to show how you got an answer. Don't cross out your working out until you know your answer is correct.

1 Mustafa worked out that

$15 + 12 = 27$.
How did he get this answer?

2 Isabel calculated that

$32 - 9 = 23$.
How did she get this answer?

3 Lily worked out that

$5 \times 3 = 15$.
How did she get this answer?

4 Freddie found out that

$24 \div 4 = 6$.
How did he get this answer?

Challenge!

1 Ben worked out that
$15 - 3 + 4 = 16$.
Show one way he could have done this calculation.

2 Andrea worked out that
$3 \times 5 + 4 = 19$.
How could she have got her answer?

☆ Star Tips ☆

There are lots of different ways to work out calculations.
Try using some of these!

• Drawing number lines.
• Partitioning numbers for addition.
• Drawing pictures for multiplication and division.

Name: ....   Date: ....

Missing numbers, missing signs

The signs in calculations tell you what to do when solving a problem. The equals sign means that a calculation <u>balances</u>. It is the same on each side.

For example, 4 + 2 = 5 + 1   4 add 2 is the same as 5 add 1.

You can check both sums are correct as they both add up to give the answer 6.

The Sneaky Sign Stealer has stolen all the signs and some numbers.

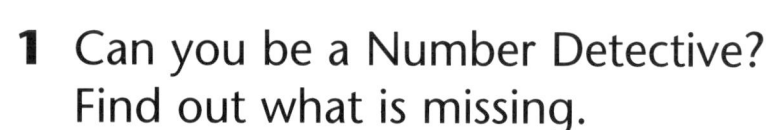

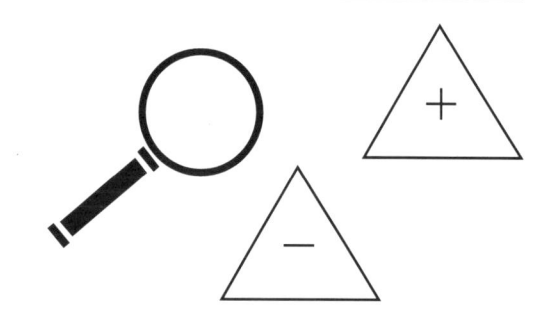

1 Can you be a Number Detective? Find out what is missing.

a 17 ☐ 3 = 14   b 5 ☐ 4 = 20   c 13 ☐ 8 = 21

d 10 ☐ 2 = 5   e 32 ☐ 2 + 30   f 10 ☐ 6 = 60

2 Now try making these sums balance.

a 10 + 5 = 12 + ☐   b 12 − 4 = 3 + ☐

c 20 ÷ ☐ = 4 − 0   d 6 × ☐ = 6 + 6

Challenge!
Find as many different ways as you can to make this sum balance.

16 + ☐ = 30 − ☐

☆ Star Tips ☆
• Some calculations start with the answer.
• Make sure both sides of the equals sign have the same answer.

© Rising Stars UK Ltd. 2004   Excellence in Word Problems   Year 2/Copymaster 15

Name: .... Date: ....

Problem solving

When solving problems, read the story very carefully and think about what it is asking you to do.

Mr Flower wanted to know how much pocket money his class got each week. The children gave him these problems to solve. Can you help him?

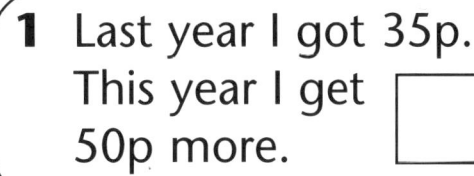

1 Last year I got 35p. This year I get 50p more. ☐

2 My sister gets £1.20. I get twice as much. ☐

3 If I had 25p more I would have 75p. ☐

4 My brother gets £1. I get half as much. ☐

5 My sister gets £2. I get 30p less. ☐

6 I get 10p a day. How much is that in one week? ☐

Challenge!
See if you can write your own clues for these amounts
1 £1 **2** 20p **3** 50p **4** £2

☆ Star Tip ☆
Underline the words that tell you what to do, such as **more**, **twice** or **as much**.

© Rising Stars UK Ltd. 2004 Excellence in Word Problems Year 2/Copymaster 16

Name: ....   Date: ....

Solving number puzzles

To solve number puzzles, look for patterns and try different ways to make the sum work. There is often more than one correct answer!

1 Put the numbers 1, 2, 3, 4 and 5 in the circles so that circles next to each other have a difference of more than one.

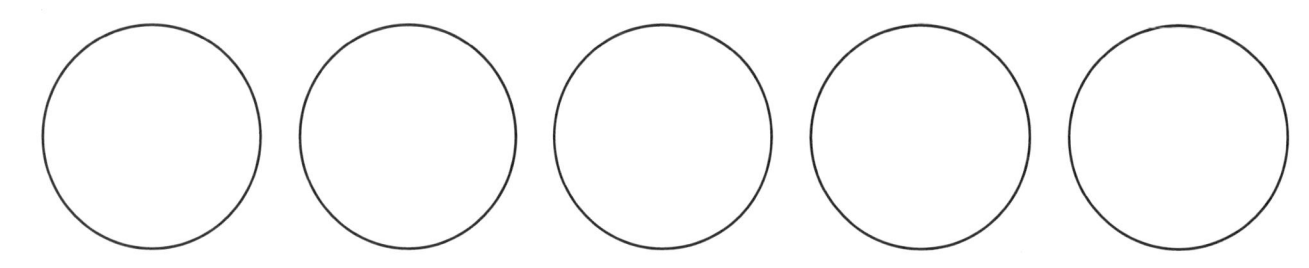

○ ○ ○ ○ ○

2 Put the numbers 1, 2, 3, 4, 5 and 6 in the circles so that each side of the triangle adds up to 12.

3 Find different ways of adding three odd numbers to make 15.

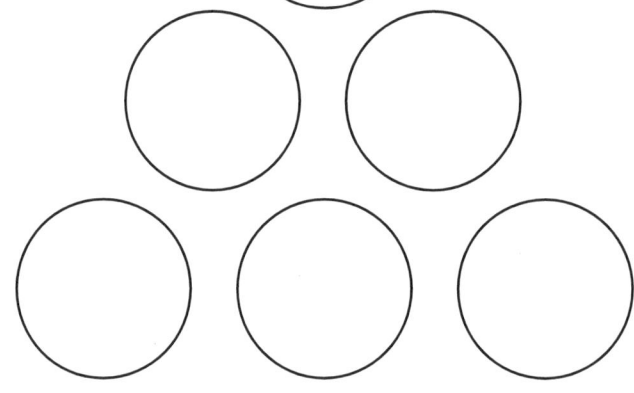

Challenge!

In this magic square each line adds up to 15. Can you put the numbers 1, 2, 3, 5, 7 and 8 in the right places? You must make the diagonal lines add up to 15, too!

		6
4	9	

☆ Star Tip ☆

Write sums to check that your answers are correct.

Solving shape puzzles

To solve these shape puzzles you need to look carefully for as many different shapes as you can. Remember, some shapes can overlap, so be careful to count correctly.

1 How many triangles can you see in this shape?

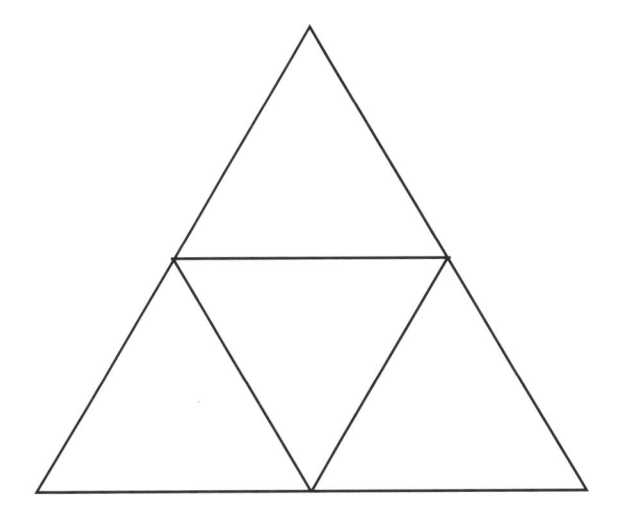

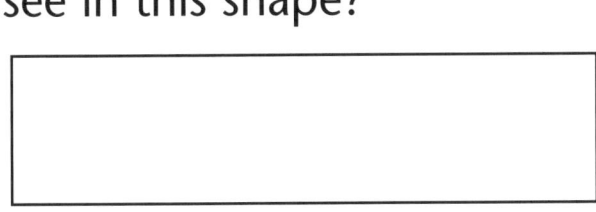

2 How many rectangles can you see in this shape?

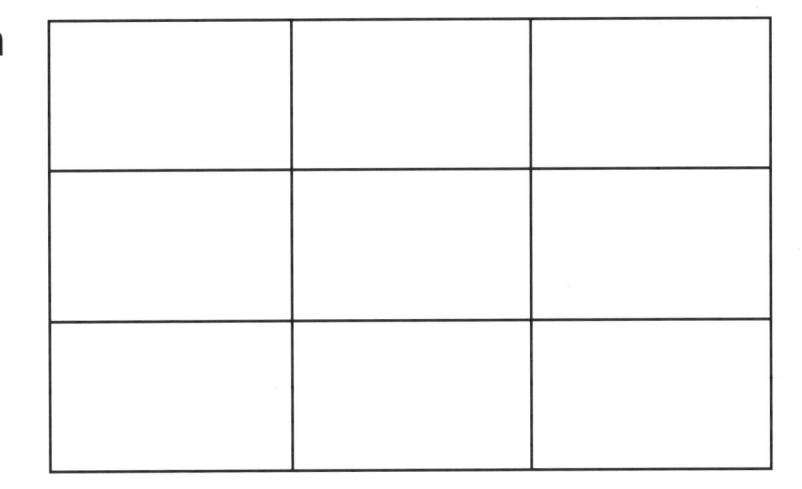

☆ Star Tip ☆
A triangle or rectangle can be made of two or more smaller shapes joined together.

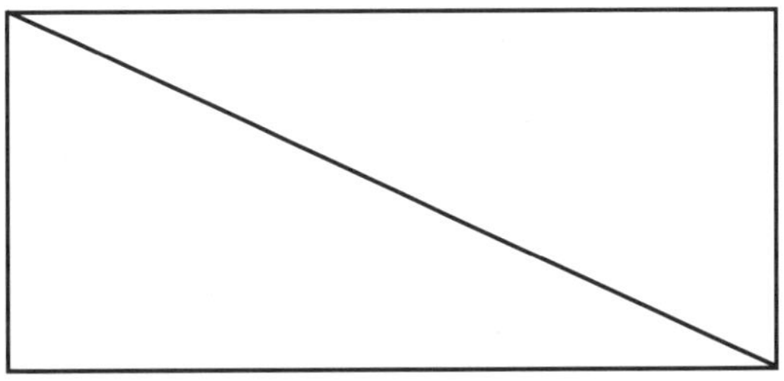

Challenge!
Use some squared paper. How many different shapes can you make using four squares? Count the number of sides.

Name: .... Date: ....

Totals of coins

You can find change by drawing a number line. If you bought a book for 35p with a 50p coin your change would be 15p.

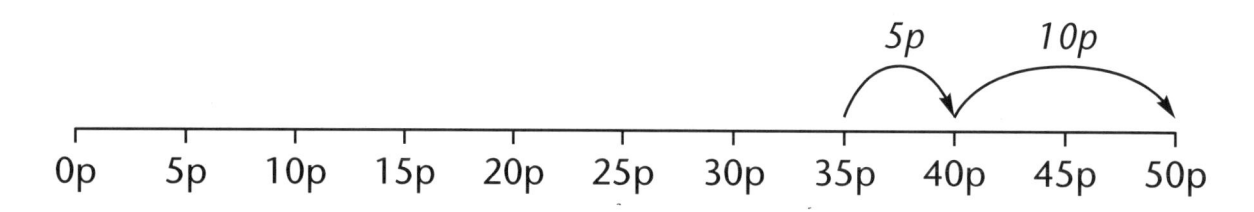

0p 5p 10p 15p 20p 25p 30p 35p 40p 45p 50p

Sita is shopping with a 50p coin. She buys two items and is given some change.
What two items could she buy? How much change would she get for each pair of things she buys?

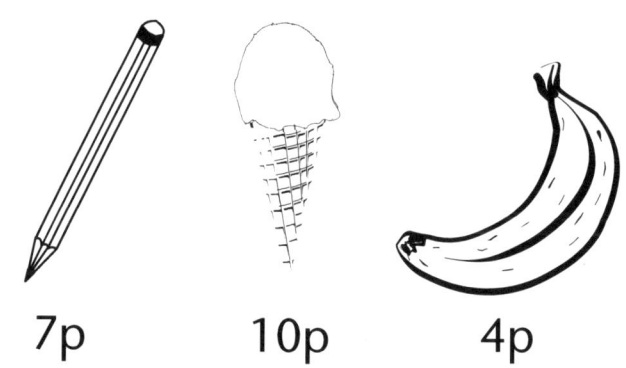

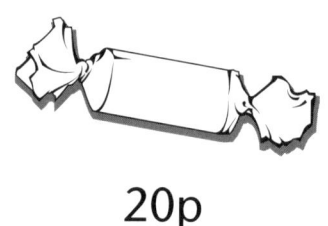

7p   10p   4p

6p   20p   5p   14p   31p

Challenge!
Sita now has £1 and can buy three items. What could she buy and how much change would she get?

☆ Star Tip ☆
To calculate the change, you need to **add** up what Sita has spent and **subtract** the answer from the amount of money she had to start.

© Rising Stars UK Ltd. 2004   Excellence in Word Problems   Year 2/Copymaster 19

Name: ....   Date: ....

Finding totals of coins

You can make the same total using different coins. For example, 20p could be 10p + 10p, or 10p + 5p + 5p.

A shopkeeper needs to give Adam 35p in change. He does not have any 1p or 2p coins.

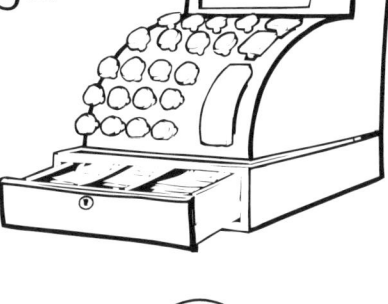

1 How can he do this using only 3 coins?

2 How about 4 coins?

3 How about 5 coins?

4 What other ways can the shopkeeper find to make 35p?

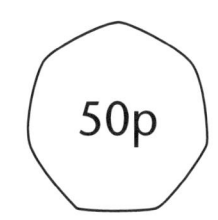

5p

10p

20p

50p

Challenge!
Find as many different ways as you can to make £1 using 5p, 10p, 20p and 50p coins. Count how many coins each way uses.

☆ Star Tip ☆
Remember, there may be more than one way to make the same total.

© Rising Stars UK Ltd. 2004 Excellence in Word Problems Year 2/Copymaster 20

Name: .... Date: ....

Time problems

Solving problems in time involves reading times on a clock and looking at the <u>hours</u> and <u>minutes</u>.

The films at a cinema start every half an hour. The cinema opens at 4 o'clock.

1 If the first film starts at 4 o'clock, what time will the next six films start?

2 Now work out how many films will have started before 6.30 p.m.?

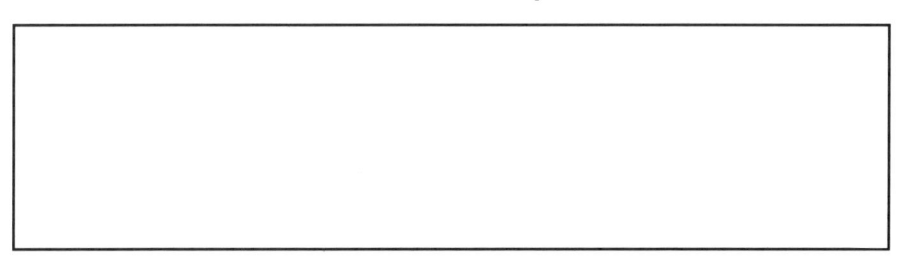

3 Harry goes into the cinema at 4.00 p.m. He comes out 6.00 p.m. How long was he in the cinema?

Challenge!
Harry had half an hour to buy his ticket and some popcorn. What time did the film start?

☆ Star Tips ☆
- Half an hour is the same as 30 minutes.
- Half past four can also be written as 4:30.

© Rising Stars UK Ltd. 2004   Excellence in Word Problems   Year 1/Copymaster 21

Name: .... Date: ....

Length problems

One of the units for measuring length is called metres, which you can write as m. You can also measure in centimetres (cm). There are 100 cm in one metre.

1 Farmer Brown has 20 metres of fence. Draw all the different square and rectangular pens he can build for his sheep. Don't forget to show how long each side is!

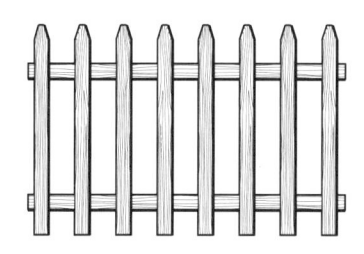

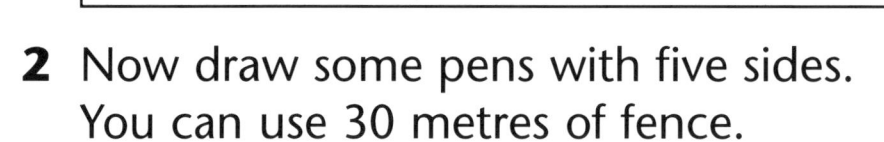

2 Now draw some pens with five sides. You can use 30 metres of fence.

Challenge!
Design some pens that have 5 or 6 sides using 20 metres of fence.

☆ Star Tip ☆
Always check that the sides of the pen add up to 20 metres.

© Rising Stars UK Ltd. 2004   Excellence in Word Problems   Year 2/Copymaster 22

Name: ....   Date: ....

Symmetrical patterns

A symmetrical pattern has a line of symmetry through its middle. One side is a <u>mirror image</u> of the other side.

The genie of a magic lamp needs to design a new flying carpet for Prince Laugh-a-Lot. The carpet has to be symmetrical or it will not fly in a straight line. Can you help the genie design some symmetrical carpets for the Prince? Colour a symmetrical pattern on each one.

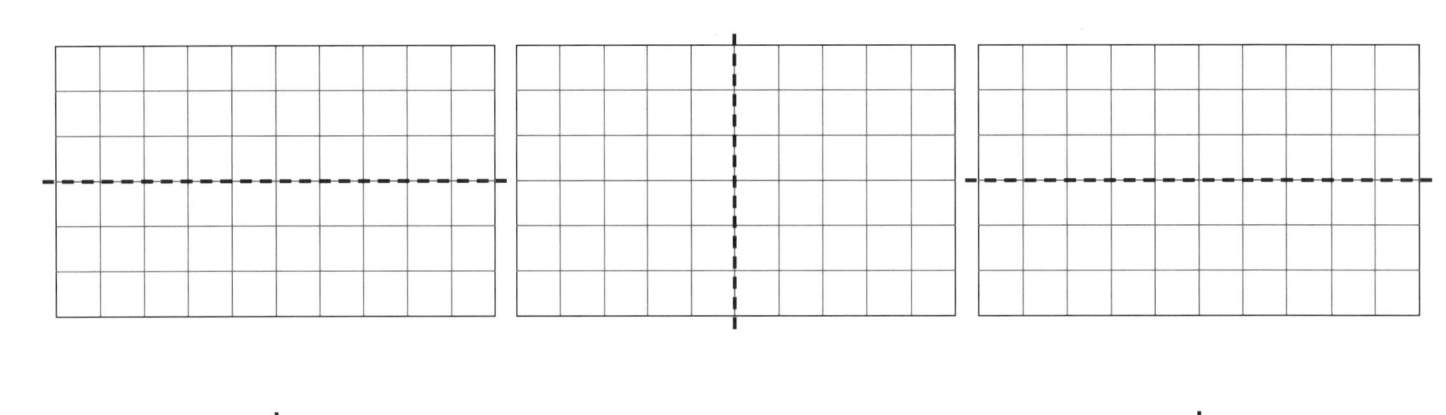

Challenge!

Prince Laugh-a-Lot was so pleased with your designs, he would like you to help him make a flying carpet with two lines of symmetry. See if you can complete this carpet.

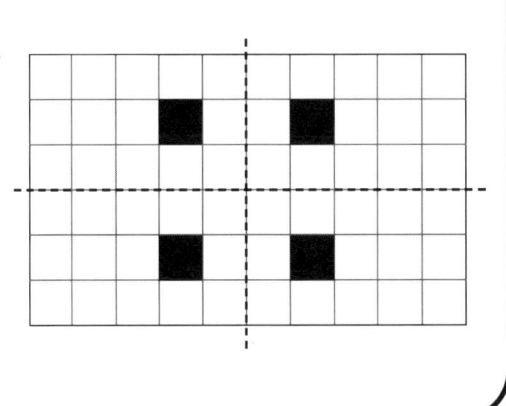

☆ Star Tip ☆

Start by colouring the squares nearest to the line of symmetry.

© Rising Stars UK Ltd. 2004   Excellence in Word Problems   Year 2/Copymaster 23

Name: .... Date: ....

Making 3-D shapes

A 3-D shape is a solid shape. It has <u>faces</u>, <u>corners</u> and <u>edges</u>. It can be made by joining 2-D shapes together.

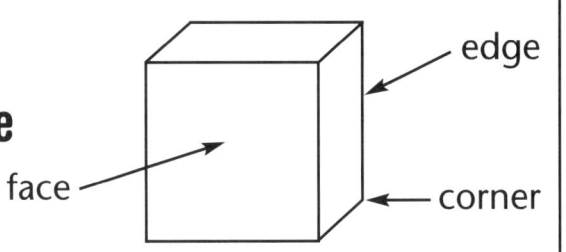

You will need some paper, scissors, masking tape and Resource copymaster 3. Build these 3-D shapes by cutting out the correct 2-D shapes and taping them together.

Cube   **Square-based pyramid**   **Cylinder**

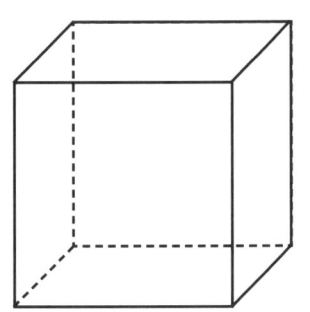

☆*Hint!*
You will need 6 shapes that are all the same.

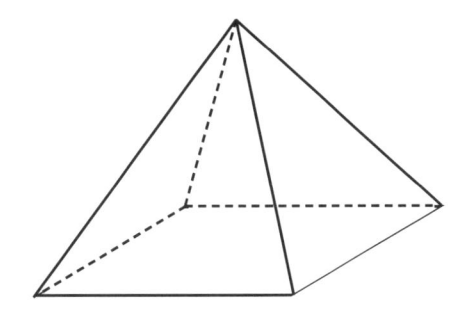

☆*Hint!*
There is a clue in its name.

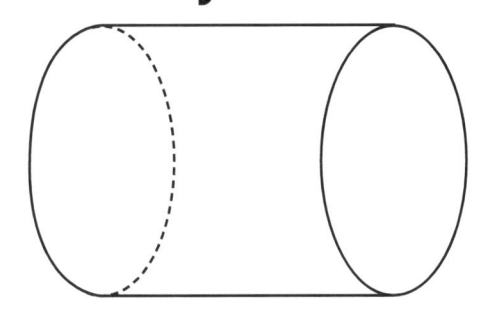

☆*Hint!*
You will only need 3 shapes for this one.

1 How many faces does each of your shapes have?

Cube ☐   Pyramid ☐   Cylinder ☐

2 How many corners does each of your shapes have?

Cube ☐   Pyramid ☐   Cylinder ☐

Challenge!
How many edges does each of your 3-D shapes have?

☆ **Star Tip** ☆
Look at the shapes of each face on the 3-D shape. Those are the shapes you will need!

© Rising Stars UK Ltd. 2004   Excellence in Word Problems   Year 2/Copymaster 24

Name: .... Date: ....

Venn diagrams

A Venn Diagram is a special type of picture that helps you sort information. It is made up of two groups, or circles, that overlap.

Can you sort the following numbers into the correct places on the Venn Diagram? Numbers that could go on either side belong in the small section in the middle.

| 15 | 44 | 33 | 21 | 7 | 26 | 11 | 32 | 27 | 45 |
| 38 | 1 | 30 | 42 | 50 | 3 | 37 | 43 | 19 | 52 |

Odd numbers   **Numbers greater than 20**

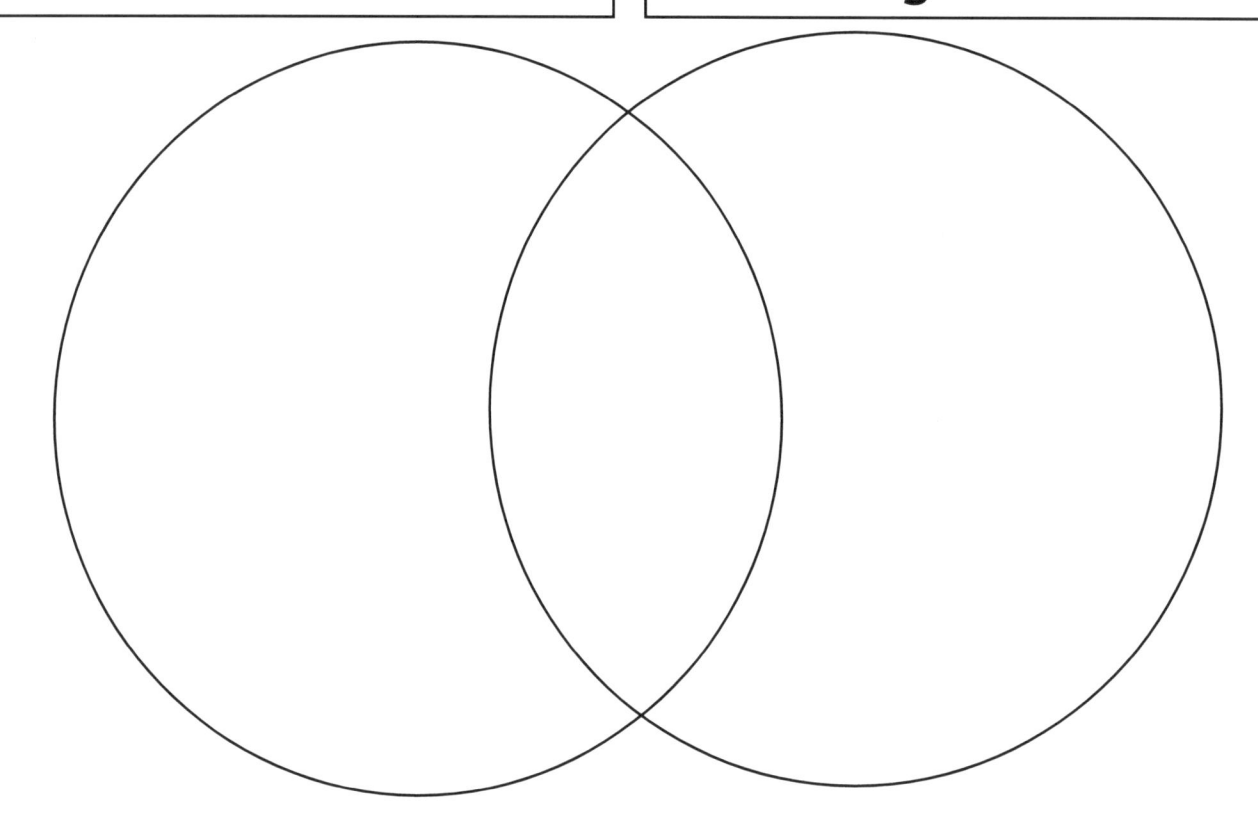

Challenge!
Can you write some numbers that would not fit in either circle?

☆ Star Tip ☆
The middle part of the Venn Diagram is for numbers that fit in **both** circles. That means odd numbers that are greater than 20!

© Rising Stars UK Ltd. 2004   Excellence in Word Problems   Year 2/Copymaster 25

Name: .... Date: ....

Presenting information

There are lots of different ways to present information, such as lists and tables. There are also special pictures you can draw to show something, such as bar charts and pictograms.

1 Class 2 were looking at what pets they had at home. Their teacher drew a table to show this information.

Pet	Number of children
Cat	8
Dog	6
Rabbit	7
Goldfish	0
Bird	5
Mouse	3

Show this information in a bar chart and a pictogram on the back of this page. Don't forget to give your bar chart and pictogram a title.

Here are examples of a bar chart and a pictogram to help you.

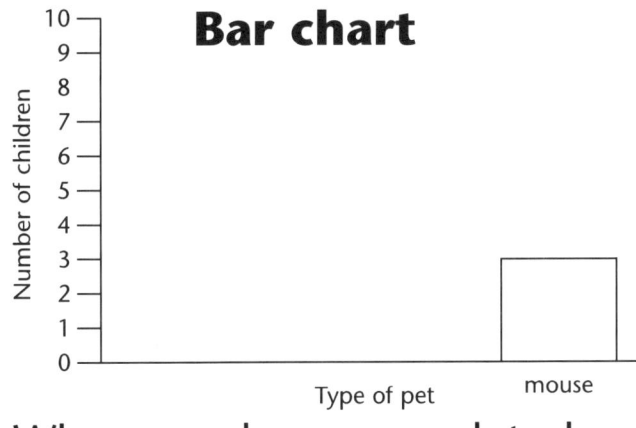

Bar chart

Pictogram

Pets	Number of children
mouse	🐭 🐭 🐭

2 When you have completed your bar chart, look at it and write down three things you notice about the information.

Challenge!

Which of these statements are true? If they are wrong, write one that is correct.
 1 More children have a dog than a bird.
 2 14 children have a cat or a dog.
 3 A rabbit is the most common pet.

☆ Star Tip ☆

When drawing a bar chart make sure you label both axes.

© Rising Stars UK Ltd. 2004   Excellence in Word Problems   Year 2/Copymaster 26

Name: .... Date: ....

Ordinal numbers

Ordinal numbers tell us the <u>order</u> of things. Use words such as <u>first</u>, <u>second</u>, <u>third</u> and <u>fourth</u>.

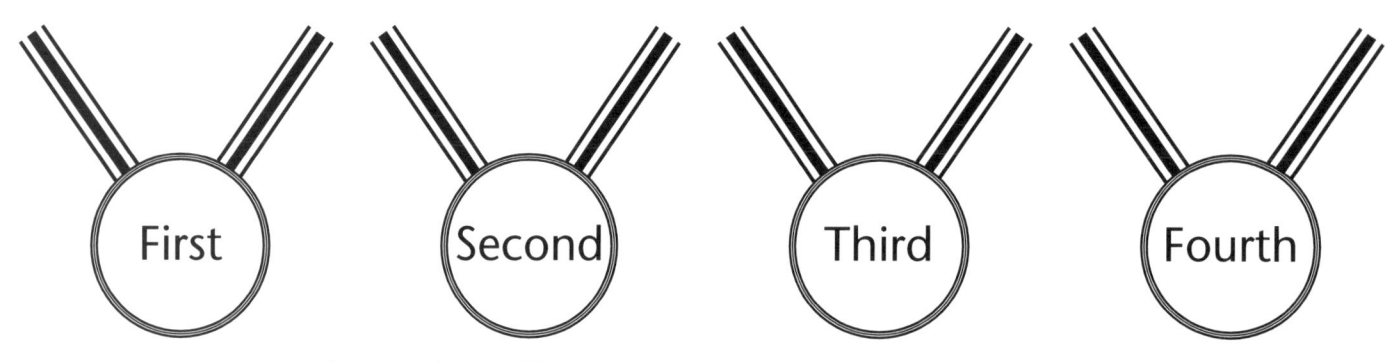

First   Second   Third   Fourth

Jess, Tom, Sarah and Holly ran some races.
Here are the results.

	Time in minutes			
	Jess	Tom	Sarah	Holly
Egg and spoon	4	3	5	6
Obstacle	7	6	4	5
Sack	5	7	6	4

1 Who came first in the egg and spoon race?

2 Who came third in the obstacle race?

3 Who came fourth in the sack race?

Challenge!
Who came second in two of the races?

☆ Star Tip ☆
- You can write ordinal words as ordinal numbers, like this:
first as **1st**
second as **2nd**
third as **3rd**
fourth as **4th**.

© Rising Stars UK Ltd. 2004   Excellence in Word Problems   Year 2/Copymaster 27

Name: .... Date: ....

Finding the difference between two numbers

You can use a number line to find the **difference** between two numbers. **Count** how many jumps there are from one number to the other. For example,

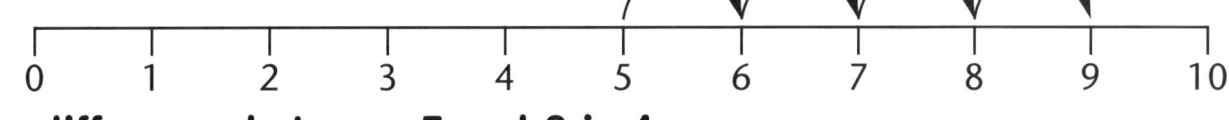

0 1 2 3 4 5 6 7 8 9 10

the difference between 5 and 9 is 4.

Sally and Mena are playing snakes and ladders. The difference between the numbers they have landed on is 8. The game goes up to 20 squares. What numbers could they be on?
Find as many different answers as you can!

Challenge!
Sally is now 15 squares in front of Mena. What numbers could they be on?

☆ Star Tips ☆
- Try counting up from the smaller number to the larger number.
- Difference means the same as take away, for example, 19 − 5 = 14.

© Rising Stars UK Ltd. 2004   Excellence in Word Problems   Year 2/Copymaster 28

Doubling and halving

Doubling is the same as **multiplying** by 2.
Halving is the same as **dividing** by 2.

1 Double all the numbers between 1 and 20.
Can you see any patterns?

| 1 | 2 | 3 | 4 | 5 | 6 | 7 | 8 | 9 | 10 |

| 11 | 12 | 13 | 14 | 15 | 16 | 17 | 18 | 19 | 20 |

2 Now try halving all the numbers to 20.
What did you find out?

| 1 | 2 | 3 | 4 | 5 | 6 | 7 | 8 | 9 | 10 |

| 11 | 12 | 13 | 14 | 15 | 16 | 17 | 18 | 19 | 20 |

Challenge!
1 What happens when you double an odd number?
2 What happens when you double an even number?

☆ Star Tips ☆
- There are some numbers that you can't halve into whole numbers!
- Try doubling the tens, then double the units, then add the two numbers together to find the answer.

© Rising Stars UK Ltd. 2004　　Excellence in Word Problems　Year 2/Copymaster 29

Name: .... **Date:** ....

Two step operations

A two step operation means there are two parts to the problem. Work out the first part of the sum. Then do the second part.

For example,   6 + 2 + 3 =

first step   6 + 2 = 8

second step   8 + 3 = 11

So the answer is 11!

Use these numbers and signs to write five different two step operations. What different answers can you make?

+   −   2   3   5   6   1   0

Challenge!
Try to write a three step problem using + and − and the 6 digits above. Now work out the answer!

☆ Star Tip ☆
Remember, always do one step at a time!

© Rising Stars UK Ltd. 2004   Excellence in Word Problems   Year 2/Copymaster 30

Name: .... Date: ....

Measuring capacity

Capacity means <u>how much liquid</u> a container holds.
It can be measured in litres or millilitres.
There are 1000 millilitres in one litre.

1 A bottle of medicine holds 25 ml. A teaspoon holds 5 ml. How many teaspoons of medicine are in the bottle?

2 A pond holds 50 litres of water. Your bucket holds 5 litres. How many buckets will you need to fill the pond?

3 Sita is having a party. There are 18 children invited. A 1 litre bottle of coke holds 4 cups. How many bottles will Sita need to buy so each child has one cup?

4 There are two containers. One holds 3 litres of water and one holds 2 litres.
   a If you fill both containers how much water will you have in total?
   b Now take the larger container and fill it twice. How much water do you have in total?

Challenge!
1 How many ml in 2 litres?
2 How many ml in 3 litres?
3 How many ml in 4 litres?
4 How many ml in $\frac{1}{2}$ litre?

☆ Star Tips ☆
- Millilitres can be written as ml.
- Litres can be written as l.
- There are 1000 millilitres in 1 litre

© Rising Stars UK Ltd. 2004   Excellence in Word Problems   Year 1/Copymaster 31

Name: .... Date: ....

Number lines

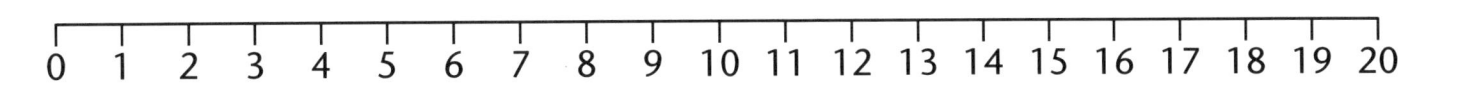

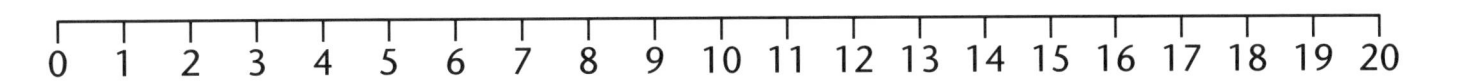

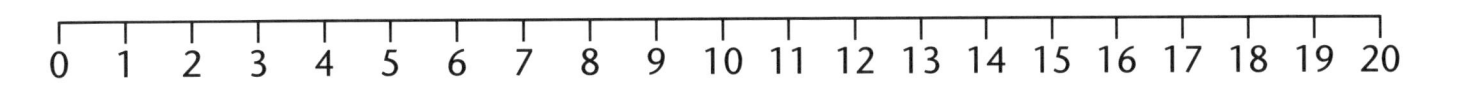

0 1 2 3 4 5 6 7 8 9 10 11 12 13 14 15 16 17 18 19 20

0 1 2 3 4 5 6 7 8 9 10 11 12 13 14 15 16 17 18 19 20

0 1 2 3 4 5 6 7 8 9 10 11 12 13 14 15 16 17 18 19 20

© Rising Stars UK Ltd. 2004   Excellence in Word Problems   Year 2/Resource Copymaster 1

Name: .... Date: ....

Clock faces

© Rising Stars UK Ltd. 2004   Excellence in Word Problems   Year 2/Resource Copymaster 2

Name: .... **Date:** ....

2-D shapes

© Rising Stars UK Ltd. 2004   Excellence in Word Problems   Year 2/Resource Copymaster 3

Name: .... Date: ....

Coins, dominoes and counters

Coins

1p	2p	5p	10p	20p	50p
1p	2p	5p	10p	20p	50p
1p	2p	5p	10p	20p	50p

Dominoes

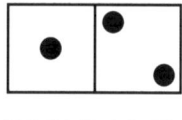

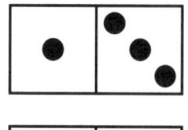

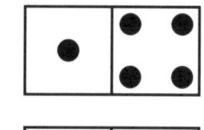

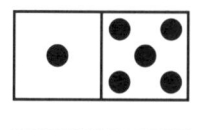

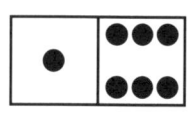

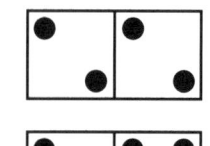

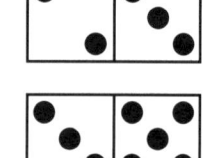

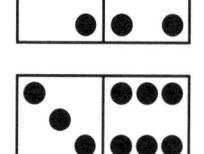

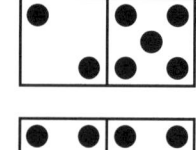

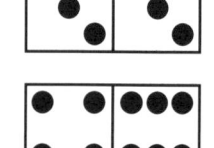

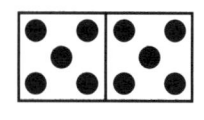

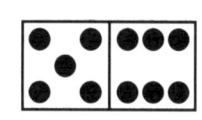

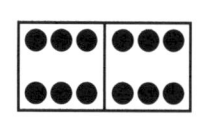

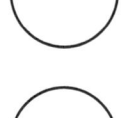

Counters

© Rising Stars UK Ltd. 2004   Excellence in Word Problems   Year 2/Resource Copymaster 4

Answers

Copymaster 1
1. 3 + 3 = 6, 5 + 5 = 10, 7 + 7 = 14
   Answers go up in 4s.
2. Answers will vary but will always be an even number.
3. Answers will vary but will always be even and two times the number added.
4. Answers will vary but will always be even.

Challenge!
When an even number is added to an odd number the answer is always odd.

Copymaster 2
1. 18, 21, 24, 27, 30 (goes up in 3s)
2. 4, 8, 12, 16, 20, 24, 28
3. Answers will vary.

Challenge!
10, 20, 30, 40, 50 and so on

Copymaster 3
1. a Check children's answers.
   b Check children's answers.
   c Check children's answers.
   d Check children's answers.
   e Check children's answers.
2. a 7.
   b 20.
   c 90 + 6.

Challenge!
Answers will vary but should have the correct hundreds, tens or units in the correct box.
1. Check children's answers.
2. Check children's answers.
3. Check children's answers.

Copymaster 4
1. Answers will vary.
2. Answers will vary.

Challenge!
479, 497, 749, 794, 947, 974

Copymaster 5
Check to see if the children are close to:
1. 7
2. 9
3. 20
4. 10

Challenge!
Check children's work.

Copymaster 6
1. 30p
2. 80p
3. 80p
4. 10p
5. 30p
6. 60p

Challenge!
Some examples are:
a 38, 42, 44
  39, 41, 43
b 56, 58, 62
  57, 59, 61
c 76, 81, 82
  79, 77, 84
d 102, 98, 104
  97, 99, 103

Copymaster 7
Answers will vary but should show quarters in each flag.

Challenge!
Answers will vary but should show thirds in each flag.

Copymaster 8
1. 5 pigs and 2 sheep
2. 4 green, 2 red and 2 orange smarties
3. 3 grapes, 3 cherries and 6 strawberries

Challenge!
$\frac{1}{2}$ have blue eyes, $\frac{1}{4}$ have green eyes and $\frac{1}{4}$ have brown eyes

45

Copymaster 9
1 Sums will vary but should show correct answers.
2 a Answers will vary.
  b 95 + 63 = 158

Challenge!
Sums will vary but should show correct answers.

Copymaster 10
1a-f Missing numbers will vary but calculations should be correct.
2 Answers will vary.

Challenge!
Missing numbers will vary but should show the correct sum.

Copymaster 11
1 3 aliens
2 3 aliens
3 9 two-headed aliens or 2 five-headed aliens and 4 two-headed aliens

Challenge!

2 heads	3 heads	5 heads
10	1	0
9	0	1
7	3	0
5	1	2
4	5	0
4	0	3
3	4	1
2	3	2
1	7	0
0	1	4
0	6	1

Copymaster 12
1 12
2 8
3 6

Challenge!
1 1
2 6

Copymaster 13
1 Wrong – answer should be 27
2 Right
3 Wrong – answer should be 20
4 Wrong – answer should be 8
5 Right
6 Wrong – answer should be 83
7 Wrong – answer should be 10
8 Right

Challenge!
1 Wrong – answer is 20
2 Right
3 Wrong – answer is 23
4 Wrong – answer is 28

Copymaster 14
Answer will vary but working should show use of appropriate methods.

Challenge!
Answers will vary.

Copymaster 15
1 a −   b ×   c +   d ÷   e =   f ×
2 a 3   b 5   c 5   d 2

Challenge!
16 + 14 = 30 − 0
16 + 13 = 30 − 1
16 + 12 = 30 − 2
16 + 11 = 30 − 3
16 + 10 = 30 − 4
16 + 9 = 30 − 5
16 + 8 = 30 − 6
16 + 7 = 30 − 7
16 + 6 = 30 − 8
16 + 5 = 30 − 9
16 + 4 = 30 − 10
16 + 3 = 30 − 11
16 + 2 = 30 − 12
16 + 1 = 30 − 13
16 + 0 = 30 − 14

Copymaster 16
1 85p
2 £2.40
3 50p
4 50p
5 £1.70
6 70p

46

Challenge!
Answers will vary.

Copymaster 17
1. 5, 3, 1, 4, 2 or
   2, 4, 1, 3, 5 or
   4, 2, 5, 3, 1 or
   4, 1, 3, 5, 2 or
   3, 5, 2, 4, 1 or
   3, 1, 4, 2, 5

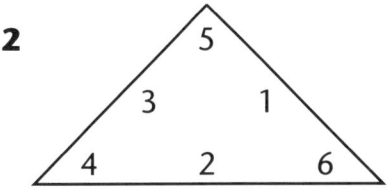

2. Triangle with 5 at top, 3 and 1 in middle row, 4, 2, 6 at bottom

3. Answers will vary but should include three odd numbers and add up to 15.

Challenge!

8	1	6
3	5	7
4	9	2

Copymaster 18
1. 5
2. 36

Challenge!
Answers will vary.

Copymaster 19
Check children's work.

Challenge!
Check children's work.

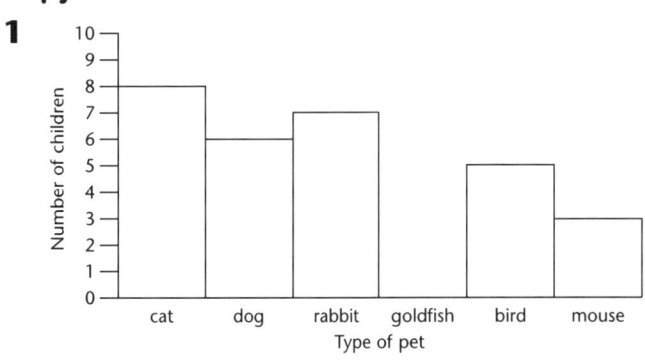

Copymaster 20
1. 20p, 10p and 5p
2. 10p, 10p, 10p and 5p or 20p, 5p, 5p and 5p
3. 10p, 10p, 5p, 5p, 5p
4. 20p, 5p, 5p, 5p or 7 5ps,

Challenge!
Answers will vary but should include only 5p, 10p, 20p and 50p and should all add to 100p or £1.00

Copymaster 21
1. 4:30, 5:00, 5:30, 6:00, 6:30, 7:00
2. 7 films will start before 8:00 o'clock
3. 2 hours

Challenge!
4.30 p.m.

Copymaster 22
1. Rectangles with sides 1×9, 2×8, 3×7, 4×6 and square 5×5 metres
2. Answers will vary – a regular shape would be 5 sides of 6 m each, but there are more possibilities if the shape is not regular, e.g. 8 m, 8 m, 8 m, 3 m and 3 m

Challenge!
Answers will vary.

Copymaster 23
Patterns will vary but need to be symmetrical.

Challenge!
Patterns will vary but should include two lines of symmetry.

Copymaster 24
Cube: 6 faces, 8 corners
Square-based pyramid: 5 faces, 5 corners
Cylinder: 3 faces, 0 corners

Challenge!
Check children's work.

Copymaster 25
Odd numbers less than 20 (left hand side of Venn)
1, 3, 7, 11, 15, 19
Odd numbers greater than 20 (centre of Venn)
21, 27, 33, 37, 43, 45
Even numbers greater than 20 (right hand side of Venn)
26, 30, 32, 38, 42, 44, 50, 52

Challenge!
2, 4, 6, 8, 10, 12, 14, 16, 18

Copymaster 26
1. Bar chart showing Number of children vs Type of pet: cat 8, dog 6, rabbit 7, goldfish 0, bird 5, mouse 3

pet	number of children
cat	●●●●●●●
dog	●●●●●
rabbit	●●●●●●
goldfish	
bird	●●●●●
mouse	●●●

2 Answers will vary.

Challenge!

1 True
2 True
3 False – a cat is the most common pet

Copymaster 27

1 Tom
2 Tom
3 Tom

Challenge!

Jess

Copymaster 28

1 and 9, 2 and 10, 3 and 11, 4 and 12, 5 and 13, 6 and 14, 7 and 15, 8 and 16, 9 and 17, 10 and 18, 11 and 19, 12 and 20

Challenge!

1 and 16, 2 and 17, 3 and 18, 4 and 19, 5 and 20

Copymaster 29

1 2, 4, 6, 8, 10, 12, 14, 16, 18, 20, 22, 24, 26, 28, 30, 32, 34, 36, 38, 40
Answers increase by 2 each time.

2 $\frac{1}{2}$, 1, $1\frac{1}{2}$, 2, $2\frac{1}{2}$, 3, $3\frac{1}{2}$, 4, $4\frac{1}{2}$, 5, $5\frac{1}{2}$, 6, $6\frac{1}{2}$, 7, $7\frac{1}{2}$, 8, $8\frac{1}{2}$, 9, $9\frac{1}{2}$, 10
The odd numbers don't halve into whole numbers, or, they increase by $\frac{1}{2}$ each time.

Challenge!

1 You always get an even number
2 You always get an even number

Copymaster 30

Check answers – children can use the numbers more than once if they wish.

Challenge!

Check answers – children can use the numbers more than once if they wish.

Copymaster 31

1 5 teaspoons of medicine
2 10 buckets of water
3 5 bottles of coke
4 **a** 5 litres
   b 6 litres

Challenge!

1 2000 ml
2 3000 ml
3 4000 ml
4 500 ml